ACCORDING TO JOHN

ACCORDING TO JOHN

A Literary Reading of the Fourth Gospel

Herman Servotte

DARTON · LONGMAN + TODD

First published in Great Britain in 1994 by
Darton, Longman and Todd Ltd
1 Spencer Court
140–142 Wandsworth High Street
London SW18 4JJ

First published in Dutch by Uitgeverij Altiora-Averbode,
in 1992 under the title *Johannes Literair*. Translated from the Dutch
by Herman Servotte.

Thanks are due to Faber and Faber Ltd
for permission to quote copyright material
from *Four Quartets* by T. S. Eliot.

ISBN 0–232–52069–0

A catalogue record for this book is available
from the British Library

Phototypeset by Intype, London
Printed and bound in Great Britain by
Page Bros, Norwich

CONTENTS

INTRODUCTION

IT SEEMS HARDLY possible to read a gospel as if it had been newly written. Centuries of exegesis and loving study have produced a hoard of commentaries, interpretations, meditations, sermons, reflections, adaptations and translations into numerous languages. The bibliography is forbiddingly large; and even if one ignored all the studies and articles it contains, one could not avoid being influenced by the cultural climate with its views on these basic texts. When presented with a gospel most people would probably think they knew what to expect. Reading it, they might have to adjust their opinions, but that would only confirm the fact that no reading of a gospel can be innocent. There is too much knowledge in the air for a morning-fresh, Adamic approach. Yet, it is such an approach that I want to try out in these pages.

My aim is to present the Gospel of St John as if it was a literary text and analyse it with the help of concepts and techniques that are used in literary studies. Over the last fifty years our understanding of the ways in which literature actually works has been greatly enhanced, and our methods of analysis have been refined accordingly. It is now possible to choose among diverse approaches, each of which will yield valuable pieces of information. The New Critic with his great respect for the 'words on the page' has taught us the importance of the linguistic choices an author has made. The Structuralists have drawn our attention to a small number of basic structures of plot and meaning underlying the apparently endless variety of stories. Deconstruction shows how language influences our thoughts, and how the signifiers tend to disrupt the text's smooth surface and create a tension between

1

contrary meanings which the author never intended. Reader-reception theories and overtly ideological forms of criticism (Marxist, feminist, black) stress the role of the reader and they have, together with deconstruction, shaken our faith in a unique meaning which would inhere in a text once and for all. There is no point in going into all the technicalities here; but the reading of the Gospel that is offered will nevertheless be guided by some awareness of the problems and the methods as they are seen by these forms of literary scholarship.

It may be useful, at this point, to spell out some of the assumptions that underlie this literary reading of the Gospel of St John. First and foremost is the option to read the text without considering the question of its historical truth. While acknowledging the importance of such a question, I want to limit myself deliberately to studying the meaning of the text and the ways in which it is created. I believe that the selection of words, of turns of phrase, of events told or of narrative devices, and the sequence in which they are recorded are of paramount importance for our understanding of the Gospel. This is not a claim that attention to these stylistic aspects will lead to the discovery of the writer's intention. What matters is what the text is seen to say, independently of the intention which is, anyhow, irretrievable. Nor is this a claim that an approach which does not stop at the words but moves towards an understanding of what actually happened has no validity; but a greater awareness of the nuances of the text may make the picture John paints of the Lord more vivid and thus contribute to a more realistic understanding of him.

This commentary does not aim at completeness; it is not meant as a line-by-line commentary, but rather as an overall view based on a literary awareness. As such, it does not touch upon questions of spirituality or the life of faith. It is meant to provide a basis on which to build a life of faith.

Three more points ought to be mentioned. First, a comparison between John's Gospel and the Synoptic Gospels will often prove illuminating. They were indeed written at an earlier date, and John's Gospel clearly supposes that his readers were familiar with them, as I hope to show later; whenever he differs from them, the personal character of his portrait of Jesus will show. Secondly, John and the other evangelists were steeped in the Jewish tradition, and many events or sayings acquire a greater depth when they are placed in the Old Testament context. Thirdly, the Gospels were written for the benefit of existing Christian communities which had, as we know from The Acts, their own forms of worship and of teaching; again, John seems to imply a readership for which allusions to, say, the Eucharist would immediately be recognized and understood.

Here, then, are the references you will need as you begin reading this book: the text of John's Gospel, the Synoptic Gospels, the Old Testament and The Acts. *The RSV Interlinear Greek–English New Testament* (Marshall Pickering, 1988) is the edition that I have used whenever special difficulties arose. But any version of the Bible may be used and is indeed better than no version at all. The text of the Gospel must take pride of place.

PROLOGUE (1:1–18)

BEFORE RELATING the events in Jesus' life, John devotes a few lines to a general introduction. Its tone is solemn, and its structure deliberately repetitive. Consider the first two verses. They can be arranged as if they belonged to a poem:

> In the beginning was *the Word*
> And *the Word* was with GOD
> And GOD was *the Word*
> *He* was in the beginning with GOD.

Obviously, lines 1 and 3, and 2 and 4 rhyme. The fact is even more striking when one realizes that the normal word-order of line 3 ('the Word was God') has been replaced by the present one ('God was the Word'), which emphasises the parallelism and its chiasmic structure. The next lines show a similar structure: 'All things through him became, and without him became not one thing which has become.' Again, the order A-B (things – he) has been inverted to B-A (he – not one thing); to formulate this differently, the affirmative first half of the sentence is followed by a negative formulation which does not, in any way, introduce a new meaning.

This type of writing is characteristic of many Old Testament texts, such as the Psalms; 'The heavens are telling the glory of God; and the firmament proclaims his handiwork' (Psalm 19) is a good example of this heavily redundant style. A related stylistic feature is the straightforward repetition of a word or a phrase, sometimes in conjunction with another, less immediately apparent, form of repetition, viz. the replacement

4

of a word through a near-synonym: thus, in verses 4 and 5: 'In him was *life*, and the *life* was the *light* of men, and the *light* shines in the *darkness* and the *darkness* did not overcome it.' The reader who is interested in this stylistic trait will find similar examples in the rest of the Prologue. Thus in verses 8ff. one gets the following word-chain: 'He (A) came, to bear witness (B), to bear witness (B) to the light (C); He (A) was not the light (C), but that he might bear witness (B) to the light (C). The light (C) that enlightens (C) was coming . . . into the world (D); it was in the world (D), and the world (D) was made through him and the world (D) knew it not.' When we replace the repeated terms by letters a clear pattern emerges: ABBC, ACBC, CCDDDD.

Closely related to the stylistic feature of repetition is the insistent use of key-words. Although the text is fairly short, it contains no less than six instances of *egeneto* (came into being). This word is used in connection with the creation of the world (vv.3–4, 10), with the coming of the Baptist (v.6), the coming of Christ (v.14) and the giving of 'grace and truth' (v.17). Given emphasis by its early position in v.6 ('Arose a man'), it is also underscored by related forms or words like *gegonen* (has become), *gennesthai* (to become), *monogenès* (only begotten); see vv.3, 15, 12, 14, 18. The impression that is thus created is one of a succession of related events. The opening words 'in the beginning', which repeat the first words of Genesis, call up the background of eternity against which the historical events are projected: becoming as opposed to being; the new in contrast with what has always been since the world 'became'. Through the use of the same word for the creation of the world, for the coming of the Baptist, and for the Incarnation of Christ the continuity of God's activity is highlighted.

The reaction to these events is indicated by another key-word *elabon-elabomen* and its cognates *katelabon-parelabon* (see vv.5, 11, 12, 16) which can all be rendered by 'receive'. Here the attitudes diverge: whereas many refuse to receive these events, the writer and the group to which he belongs have accepted them. It is important to see that the writer of the Fourth Gospel presents himself as the spokesman of a group – he speaks in the name of 'we all' (v.16) – which has already accepted the Good News. His text is destined for people who already know what he will be talking about as they share the experience of having received God's grace (see vv.14 and 16). That the text is intended for such an audience probably explains why the name of Jesus Christ, who is the central figure in the Prologue as well as in the whole Gospel, is not mentioned until verse 17, even though he is the subject right from the beginning. This Prologue, then, presupposes the faith of the audience and it is couched in a style that is strongly reminiscent of Old Testament poetry.* It presents itself as a lyrical expression of faith rather than as a dogmatic statement, as suggestive speech rather than as a doctrinal definition. We shall read the text accordingly.

Whereas the Synoptic Gospels place the beginning of Jesus' activity in historical time, John with great daring begins his account in eternity, in the beginning before the beginning of the world. The Word is at the origin of everything. The term is enigmatic, and might therefore arouse speculation. But bearing in mind that, on the one hand, it has not yet the precise meaning which it was to acquire over centuries of theological thought and that, on the other hand, the audience was familiar with the Old Testament, we shall do well to try to find out what an average member of the audience might think when confronted with the term. The word of God plays an important role in the Old Testament. It is, in the story of creation, the expression of God's creative power which calls the creation into being by naming it: 'Let there be light'. It is, in the experience of Moses, God's self-revelation when he speaks from the burning bush and answers Moses' question, 'What is your name?' It is, for the Jewish people, the pledge of the Covenant between him and his people. It is, through the Prophets, the consolation and the challenge of the Promise. It creates man, it promulgates the law, it calls upon man to serve God, it consoles and chastises, it forgives and heals, it reveals God's name, that is,

* For other examples, see Appendix 2.

his being. Therefore, this text associates the Word with life and light; it is the presence of God in the world.

In stark contrast with this divine reality, there is the world of man. It is indicated by the words 'darkness' (v.5), the Greek *kosmos* (vv.9, 10) and 'his own' (v.11). There is a certain ambivalence here. The word 'darkness' is the opposite of 'light' which belongs to the divine, and as such it seems to be an enemy of God; as v.6 has it: 'The light shines in the darkness, and the darkness has not overcome it.' The words *kosmos* and especially 'his own', however, seem more neutral; they refer to a reality which has been created by God and belongs to him by right even if in the present situation it 'knew him not' (v.10) and 'received him not' (v.11). This indeterminacy also affects the word *sarx* (v.14), which originally meant the body but gradually acquired more negative connotations as the 'seat of the passions', 'man in his mortality and his temporariness', and even – in Saint Paul – 'sinful man'. In the Prologue itself, the syntactic parallelism of verse 13 seems to equate 'blood', 'man' and 'flesh' as so many aspects of one basic reality. *Sarx* is, then, at the antipodes of the divine; and it might be said to hide the divine rather than reveal it. Therefore John creates an audacious paradox when he joins the two in the formula *Logos sarx – Verbum caro –* Word flesh' (v.14). For he weds the divine and the human, the eternal and the temporal, the power and the weakness.

That he knew what he was doing in connecting them so closely, is borne out by the choice, immediately after the paradox, of the Greek word *eskènoosen* to indicate Christ's dwelling among us. It means 'to tabernacle' and it refers to the tent sanctuary (the tabernacle) which was for the Israelites the place where God was with them; similarly, Jesus is, as will be amply shown in the further development of the story, that tabernacle. In his humanity he takes over the functions of the Word: he brings about a new creation (Cana) with a new temple ('in truth and spirit') and a new birth (Nicodemus); he forgives and heals in the name of God; he feeds the multitudes; he is the light and the life of the world; he reveals God's most inward being when dying on the cross

7

– all in the unprepossessing *sarx*, the least likely place for God's revelation.

Those who have believed in Jesus have been transformed; they have become children of God. It is important to notice the use of the term *egeneto* in this context. The term which was used for the beginning of creation, for the advent of John the Baptist, and for the coming of Christ, is used here in connection with the new life Christ gave to his followers; these are the all-important historical events. This new life has to do, on the one hand, with what the believers saw (they 'beheld his glory', v.14) and with what they heard him explain (the Greek term is *exègèsato*, v.18) about the Father, and, on the other hand, with what the believers have received through Christ, viz. 'grace upon grace' (v.16) and 'grace and truth' (v.17). At this stage, these terms largely remain abstractions, and they will have to be elucidated in our further reading of the Gospel. But already we can surmise that there will be three possible topics for the Gospel to develop: a description of the glory of Christ which they have seen; a revelation of God the Father about whom they have heard; and an insight into the new state of man who has become, in their experience, a new creature.

THE FIRST WEEK (1:19—2:11)

A FTER THE PROLOGUE which focuses on the eternal origin of the Word made flesh, John turns to the historical events which inaugurate Jesus' public life: the predication of John the Baptist, the meeting with the first disciples, and the first manifestation of Jesus' glory at the wedding at Cana. This section of the Gospel is rounded off with the statement that this was the first of the signs and that his disciples believed in him (v.11). 'After this he went down to Capernaum', a change of place which indicates the beginning of a new section. For our analysis we now limit ourselves to 1:15—2:11, which is indeed a chronological and thematic unit.

The Time Structure

Very precise time-indications are a salient feature of this section. The phrase 'the next day' occurs three times and scans the story (see 1:29, 35, 43). For the first meeting of the disciples with Jesus the moment is indicated with absolute precision: 'it was about the tenth hour' (v.39). The wedding at Cana occurs 'on the third day' (2:1); that is a time-indication which the gospels always use in connection with the Resurrection of Jesus. As we shall see later, this Gospel does not, in its later sections, seem to set great store by a precise chronology. All the more reason, then, why we should look with care at the insistent use of time indicators in this section. What are its effects on our understanding of the text?

In the Prologue John the Baptist's predication is not placed explicitly at a precise moment in time; on the contrary, in verse 15 his activity is mentioned in the present tense, as if it

9

were still going on at the moment this gospel was written, in a kind of timeless present. But then the camera zooms in on him and locates him in time 'when the Jews sent priests and Levites' (v.19), and in space 'in Bethany beyond the Jordan' (v.28). Then follow three days of growing revelation of Christ: 'the next day' (v.29) John points at Jesus, calling him the Lamb of God'; 'the next day' two of John's disciples follow Jesus 'at about the tenth hour' (v.35). From then on the Baptist's part seems to be played out. Now it is John's disciples who bear witness to Jesus; it is Andrew who tells Simon about him (vv.40–2), and Philip, who has been called by Jesus himself 'on the next day', who tells Nathanael (vv.43–5). To Nathanael Jesus promises that he 'shall see greater things than these . . . heaven opened, and the angels of God ascending and descending upon the Son of man.' (vv.50–1). That promise is fulfilled when Jesus shows his glory at Cana on the third day. There are, then, seven days from the moment when the Baptist is seen in activity to the revelation of the glory of Jesus. When one remembers that the Prologue's opening words 'in the beginning' are exactly the same words as those introducing the seven days of creation in Genesis, one cannot but think that a mirror-effect is intended here. It is as if the text wanted to suggest that a new creation has come into being, or at least that there is a relationship between the first creation and the coming of Jesus.

The Theme of Seeing

In a text which stresses the importance of 'witnessing' one would expect a frequent use of the word 'to hear' and its cognates. The fact that the Prologue speaks about Jesus as 'the Word' can only bolster this expectation. And indeed the word 'hear' is used, but not as often as one would have expected: the disciples 'hear' the Baptist speak about Jesus (v.37), Simon hears from Andrew, and Nathanael from Philip. Instead, the dominating word is that of 'seeing, beholding, looking'. The Baptist draws attention to Jesus ('behold', v.29), he 'saw the Spirit descend' (v.32) and he repeats 'he has seen' (v.34); the disciples whom Jesus 'sees' following him (v.38) are invited to 'come and see' (v.39); Philip invites Nathanael to 'come and see' (v.46); Jesus sees Nathanael and promises that he shall 'see' greater things (v.51). While acknowledging the importance of the witness whose words can be heard, the text seems to attach more importance to man's personal experience of Jesus; and our further reading will confirm this hypothesis.

What is it they see? In order to answer this question, we look once more at the behaviour of the Baptist. His words are characterized by negation. To each question from the Jews, he gives a negative answer: 'I am not the Christ, not the prophet, not Elijah' (vv.20–1). Not only does he openly acknowledge that he is inferior to Christ, but he also upsets the expectations of the Jews. They had their preconceived ideas about the Messiah and about what would precede his coming, but John's answers do away with all their certainties. Even his apparently straightforward answers concerning the Messiah remain mysterious. He speaks of a third person, but does not call him by his name; neither does he define what the third man is. Descriptions of the type 'one whom you do not know' (v.26), 'he who comes after me' (v.27), are hardly illuminating; they are as puzzling as the metaphor 'Lamb of God' or the predicateless assertion 'before me he was' (v.30). One has the impression that the Baptist avoids giving too much information; he acts as if he wanted to create an open mental space for the Messiah to appear and to be seen, independently of the viewer's preconceptions.

And indeed, after verse 36 John disappears from the Gospel, only to reappear briefly in chapter 3 (v.25ff). Now it is Jesus himself who enters the scene; him they must see and come to know. That moment is so important that it gets mentioned as the 'tenth hour', not so much because the apostles were overwhelmed (that would be a psychological interpretation) but because that is the moment when the history of Christ's self-revelation begins. The Synoptic Gospels inaugurate their story with the birth of Jesus or, like Mark, with his baptism; John's Gospel begins on earth as soon as Jesus shows himself. There must indeed be a preparation in so far as others, a John the Baptist or one of the disciples, talk about Jesus and show the way to him, but in the final analysis each individual must decide for himself. In the words of the Gospel, each person must come and see where Christ stays. In this light it is remarkable that the disciples are not called by Christ as they are in the other Gospels. Here, only Philip is told, 'Follow me' (v.43). The others are drawn by what they see and might discover.

As indicated before, the group for whom John writes his Gospel is made up of believers who have already received the fullness of the Good News; they have seen Christ (v.14), and they see in him the Son of the Father. They are, therefore, ahead of the disciples whose life of faith is only just beginning. At the outset of their lives of faith the disciples call Jesus, 'Rabbi' (v.38), 'the Messiah' (v.41), 'the one of whom Moses ... wrote' (v.46). Nathanael seems to be one step ahead, in that he calls Jesus, 'Son of God' (v.49). But it is a moot point whether that term is meant to carry the full weight which it was to acquire later. One should notice that the term is followed by the title 'King of Israel', which, coming as it does at the end of a series of similar terms, is, according to all the laws of rhetoric, the higher title. If the 'Son of God' was the higher title, it would stand in a stylistically awkward position. Moreover, Jesus promises to show them even more; how could he do that if his divine nature had already manifested itself? We shall, therefore, do well to accept the term in a non-technical way, and read it with the meaning it has in, for example, the Psalms. If the disciples have not yet understood what they have seen, the function of Cana becomes apparent; it deepens their incipient faith, as we shall see in a moment.

One more point ought to be made. In the order in which the disciples come to Jesus, there is again a difference when compared with the Synoptic Gospels. There, Simon is given pride of place, here it is Andrew and one whose name is not mentioned. Similar changes of order are too frequent in this Gospel not to have been deliberate. For the intended first audience there is a special relation between Jesus and the anonymous disciple; and that special relationship is stressed whenever there is a chance to do so. Yet, Peter is always given his due; here he is not the first to see the Lord, but he receives a new name that has a bearing on his later functions in the Church.

To summarize: the author of the Gospel introduces himself as the spokesman of a group who have received the fullness of faith in Christ. From this vantage-point he will describe how Jesus manifested his glory and how the disciples came to believe in him. The Baptist's role in this process is vital, because the Spirit has revealed to him who Jesus is (v.32). Yet, the Baptist's mission is of a temporary nature. He retires from the scene as soon as Jesus appears and invites the disciples to 'come and see'; they, for their part, give their faith to him. In this twofold process the wedding at Cana represents a high point. It concludes the first week of Jesus' activity which began, after the preparatory work by the Baptist, at about the tenth hour near Bethany beyond the Jordan. The Word of God has become flesh, firmly anchored in our history.

The First Sign: Cana, the Bridegroom of the New Covenant

Cana, says the Gospel, is the place where 'Jesus manifested his glory, and his disciples believed in him' (2:11). But at the same time it stresses the fact that 'his hour has not yet come' (2:4). This expression is always used to indicate the passion and glorification of Jesus. We are then asked to look upon what happened at Cana, both as the revelation of his being and as an anticipation of a greater event that is still to come. That is tantamount to saying that Cana is a sign in more than one sense: it reveals something valid about Jesus and it is, therefore, a sign of the hidden reality of his being; but it is also a sign of another sign, namely the crucifixion which, in this Gospel, is the supreme revelation.

But if it is a sign, the question arises, what is its signifier? The transformation of water into wine? That is unlikely, if only because of the secondary, subsidiary position to which this fact is relegated. It is mentioned as if by accident in the phrase 'the water now become wine' (2:9). Clearly, the signifier must be found elsewhere – in the whole story. If we try out that hypothesis, we must first become aware of the story's

13

astonishing features. Here is a list of them, in the form of questions. Why does Mary intervene? Why does Jesus snub her and, a moment later, take charge of the situation? Why are there six water-pots and why must they first be filled with water; Why the detour over the water-pots? Why does nobody, except the servants, know the origin of the wine? Why does the steward's question to the bridegroom receive no answer? And, the most urgent question: In what sense can Jesus have manifested his glory if only the servants are privy to what has really happened? These questions are all the more pressing as the story is related by John only, so that one cannot find help in the other gospels.

The fact that the story takes place at a marriage may be significant. Indeed, in the Jewish tradition marriage is a symbol of the covenant between God and his people. Israel is the bride, God the bridegroom; and when Israel is unfaithful, it is accused of adultery. Examples can be found in Isaiah (54:4), Jeremiah (2:2 and 20), Ezekiel (16:1–43) and especially Hosea (chs.1–3). Moreover, at the end of the world, God will invite his chosen to a feast on the holy mountain, with the choicest food and rich wines. The bridegroom at the present wedding is unable to bring about the fullness of the symbol, as he runs out of wine; the feast threatens to peter out. At this point Jesus intervenes, thereby earning the title of the true bridegroom (a title the Baptist uses for him in 3:29). His wine takes the place of the waters of purification, which represent the Jewish rites and the Jewish religion. That explains the detour; the water drawn from the well might have been served straightaway to the guests, but in that case it would not have become clear that the jars of purification and what they represent had been replaced. Neither the steward nor the bridegroom are aware of these facts; but the servants who are here called *diakonoi* (deacons, an unusual but typically Christian name) know about the wine and its origin. They, and they only, can draw the right conclusion that Jesus is the true bridegroom.

The important thing, then, is not the transformation of the water into wine, but Jesus effectively taking charge of the feast which singles him out as the true bridegroom, God's representative. His action sets the stage for a new form of relationship between God and his people. This new stage is not reached because of a human demand, nor even because of his mother's demand; it is entirely due to God's initiative or, to be more precise, to Jesus' decision in conformity with God's will. But even if this is a moment of revelation, it is not yet the final revelation, but merely an anticipation, and the first one, of the hours on the cross. As Mary will be standing under the cross, it is fitting that she should also be present at this first, anticipatory sign. Even if Jesus' action is not prompted by her words, she tells the servants to do whatever he may ask them; that manifests her faith in him. She is, in this Gospel, the first to offer evidence of such faith.

This reading of the marriage at Cana, taken together with the results of the analysis of the time structure, highlights the importance of the first week in John's Gospel. It is like a new creation; and the essence of what can be said about Christ is already given. And yet, the reader also awaits further explanations. In what sense does Jesus bring about a new creation? What is it that the disciples will have to discover when his hour has come? What are the other signs, if this is the first? And what will they add to our understanding of Jesus?

THE TIME OF THE SIGNS

THE SECOND SIGN: WORD OF RENEWAL
(2:12—4:54)

THE TIME-INDICATION *meta tauta* (afterwards) closes an episode and opens up a new one. Here (2:12) it introduces a passage about the cleansing of the temple and the encounter with Nicodemus. Another *meta tauta* in 3:28 ushers in Jesus' return journey to Galilee, an ultimate witness of John the Baptist, the passage about the Samaritan woman and the story of the healing of the official's son. As this healing is called the 'second sign' (4:54) and as it is explicitly linked with Cana (4:46) it seems logical to consider the whole text between the first and the second sign as one unit, the more so as the second sign seems to be thematically related to what is revealed in that section of the Gospel. (For further justification of this division, see Appendix 1.)

The Temple Cleansed: the New Temple

In sharp contrast with the Synoptic Gospels, John places this episode at the very beginning of Jesus' public life. It is his first reported public action after Cana. Why John chooses to present it at this stage is fairly obvious. He wants to represent the mission of Jesus in one striking image. Now that mission is, as Cana has shown, the replacement of the old religion by the new one. The cleansing of the temple repeats this statement in a new key. One might think that the dealers and changers are engaged in lawful activities but that they have encroached on the space or on the hours of day allotted to

16

them. If such were the case, Jesus would be merely redressing an abuse. But that, precisely, is the point; their business within the precincts of the temple is not legitimate, even though the Jewish form of worship seems to need their presence. In order to worship, the Jews sacrifice animals. By chasing out of the temple those who deal in them, Jesus destroys the temple economy; effectively, he renders worship impossible and turns the temple into a useless building. That explains why a new temple will be needed. Answering the Jews who question his authority and right to what he has done, Jesus speaks of the new temple that he will raise up in three days (2:19). He is not understood, but he means himself. By calling himself the temple, he changes the meaning of words in a radical way. At first he is only using a metaphor, but as he is the real temple, all the other temples of stone or wood can, from now on, be called temples in a metaphorical sense only.

This double movement is typical of many New Testament sayings. Words denoting a human reality are used for a divine reality, which turns them into metaphors. But then it becomes clear that their full meaning is to be found in the human realities by analogy only. Thus, the word 'father' used in connection with God, is at first a metaphor. But as, for the New Testament, God is the only Father (see Ephesians 3:14), all humans fathers are named after him and are fathers in an analogical sense only. What happens in the language, however, is but the expression of a profound transformation of reality. The Jewish religion and the temple, which is its symbol, have to make way for the new religion with the Christ as its central figure. This message links this episode with Cana where Jesus revealed himself as the new bridegroom; and it also connects it with Jesus' conversation with the Samaritan woman where both the Jewish and Samaritan places of worship are declared obsolete and replaced by worship in 'spirit and truth'.

This substitution apparently can not be brought about without violence. Jesus himself uses a whip to drive out the sellers, he pours out the coins of the money-changers and he overturns their tables. His violence is justified by the 'zeal for God's house' which consumes him. That verb 'consume' can be understood in two ways; in its figurative sense it means that the zeal for God's house is Jesus' overriding concern, but in its literal sense it means that the zeal for God's house devours and kills him. Both meanings obtain here; and it is no accident that this event takes place around the Jewish Passover, which will also be the time of Jesus' violent death on the cross. Jesus' violence will thus be met by another violence. But lest we attach too much importance to the well-known mechanism of action and reaction, the quotation from the Old Testament (Psalm 69:9) finds the cause of Jesus' death, not in the enmity of others but in the motivation of his own soul, the 'zeal of your house'. This manner of underscoring Jesus' independence is a frequent ploy in John: at Cana Jesus rejected his mother's plea and then proceeded to act independently, here his independence from external factors is again implied. It is as if John wanted to show the greatness of Christ, who is not only beyond human threats and human violence, but who always acts of his own free will, not influenced by others.

That can be explained by John's bifocal narrative perspective. Looking at the historical Jesus he always sees the risen Christ and he projects what is proper to the latter on to the former. Or, to formulate this differently, he tells his story from two points of view: in the main story he looks at the event through the unenlightened eyes of the participants, but in verses 17, 21 and 22 he looks at the event from the point of view of one who knows the whole story and who can interpret it in the light of the resurrection. (For more details on this subject, see Appendix 1.)

Nicodemus and the New Birth

The story of Nicodemus consists of two distinct passages. The first (3:1–10) is a conversation between Jesus and the pharisee; the second (3:11–21) is an authorial commentary.

The conversation introduces Nicodemus, the first of Jesus' three interlocutors in this section on the second sign (the other two being the Samaritan woman and the pagan official whose son Jesus heals). Nicodemus represents the official Jewish religion; his position is a dubious one. He respects

18

Jesus, calls him 'Rabbi' and asks him serious questions. But he comes by night; and in a gospel that is so rich in symbolism as John's such a detail must not be overlooked. Nicodemus later intervenes on behalf of Jesus (see 7:50–1) and assists the disciples at the burial (see 19:39–40), but at this stage he is not yet ready to understand Jesus, let alone to follow him. Jesus' ironical remark, 'You are a teacher of Israel and you can't understand this!' (3:10) underscores Nicodemus' inability to see eye to eye with Jesus.

Nicodemus does not understand Jesus' words about the necessity of a new birth. As so often in this Gospel, Jesus' interlocutor understands his words in another sense than the one intended. Here, that is what happens with the word *anothen* which can be translated as 'again' but also as 'from above'. Nicodemus is fixated on 'again' and persists in a literal interpretation which makes for pure nonsense. Jesus, however, intends both meanings: a birth 'from above' which will in effect bring into being a new creature, one that is born 'again' in a spiritual sense. The words from above refer to one pole of an opposition which appears again and again in the Gospel. 'Above' is the opposite of 'below' and refers to the world of God over against the world of man. That opposition can also be formulated in the terms 'heaven' *v.* 'earth', 'spirit' *v.* 'flesh' (3:6). One is reminded of the contrast, in the Prologue, between man born of man and man born of God. Jesus, who is the new bridegroom and who brings the new worship, is also at the source of a new life given by God. That fits in beautifully with the theme of this section of the Gospel.

Two more remarks must be made. It may seem strange that the text speaks, not of a birth of the Spirit, but of a birth of 'water and the Spirit' (3:5). But if one remembers that the early Christians used baptism to incorporate the neophytes, the difficulty vanishes. This is indeed a clear allusion to the waters of baptism out of which man arises to a new, divine life. The second remark has to do with the term 'Kingdom of God'. Together with 'Kingdom of Heaven' the term occurs very frequently in the Synoptics, but in John it is only to be found here. That seems appropriate, as Jesus is talking here to a Jew who was undoubtedly familiar with the term. As John's audience was probably less well versed in matters Jewish, he does not use the word elsewhere; by using it here in this conversation with a typical Jew where it can help characterize the scene, he shows a remarkable sense of literary decorum, using the right word in the right place.

The commentary that follows can be distinguished from the previous conversation because it refers to Jesus in the third person, as if he is not the one who does the talking. Verse 12 is the only exception. To be sure, the commentary is introduced by 'Truly, truly I say to you' (3:11), which is itself a repetition of a formula used twice by Jesus in the conversation (3:3 and 3:5), and that might strengthen the impression that it is still Jesus who is speaking. But it must be pointed out that the first-person utterance in the singular ('I') immediately switches to the plural ('we'), thus changing the text from a word of Jesus into a word about Jesus and his followers. Jesus' words about himself or the testimony of the faithful all voice the same truth.

So we shall consider the passage (3:11–21) not as a statement by Jesus but as a confession of faith in him. The sentence structure of these statements is characterized by a strict parallelism, reminiscent of the style of the Prologue.* If we replace the key phrases by capitals, the following picture emerges. Verse 16: 'For God so loved the world that he gave his Son (A) that whoever believes (B) should not perish (not-C) but have eternal life' (D); verse 17: 'For God did not send his Son (not-A) that he might judge the world (C) but that it might be saved' (D). Verse 18: '(B) is not judged' (not-C); '(not-B) has already been judged (C), because (not-B)'. Verse 19 takes up the notion of judgment. Verse 20 and 21 once again run parallel: 'every one who does evil (not-X) hates the light (Y) and does not come to the light (not-Z) lest his works are exposed' (not-ZZ); 'every one doing the truth (X) comes to the light (Z), that may be manifest' (ZZ). Verse 17 repeats verse 16, but changes into the negative; verse 21 repeats verse 20, but turns it into an affirmative statement. This typical

---

* For more examples, see Appendix 2.

style-figure drives the point home with great force, paradoxically rendering the interpretation easier.

The commentary tries to define Jesus in two ways. First, he is given titles such as 'Son of God' (16 and 18) and 'Son of Man' (13–14) the meaning of which will have to be elucidated. Second, the commentary tries to 'place' Jesus by the use of the basic oppositions we have encountered in the Prologue and in the conversation with Nicodemus. He belongs to 'heaven', that is the world of light, the realm of the spirit. In rhythmical sentences, similar to those used in the Prologue, the life and death of Jesus, the origin of his mission, its aim and its results are then briefly summarized. Once again, John blends the narrative perspective on the historical Jesus with the narrative perspective on the risen Christ; at the beginning of Jesus' public life he speaks as if Jesus had already risen from the dead; see for example, verses 18 and 19 which imply that the rejection of Jesus has already taken place. To show John's sureness of touch, attention can be drawn to his perceptive use of the theological '*dei* (must)', which is the term always used in connection with the Passion and which is here used for his 'lifting up' – a reference to his crucifixion (3:14). Baptism and cross, the giving of life by his death and the disciple's new life are thus brought together.

The text which follows (3:22—4:2) also concentrates on baptism. But it is confused. Verse 3:23 asserts that Jesus baptizes, but 4:2 denies that. One can only guess at the causes of this contradiction in so short a space. It seems probable that in his associative train of thought the mention of baptism seemed appropriate after the heavy stress on its importance for acquiring the new life in the conversation with Nicodemus. But if Jesus baptized, how then did he differ from John the Baptist? The question was pulled up short by the denial of 4:2; John even counter-attacks by reminding the readers of the Baptist's witness to Jesus. He calls him the bridegroom, which confirms our earlier reading of the sign at Cana. The verses 31–6 do not add anything new; they merely repeat with some slight stylistic variations what had been said before. They are, however, typical of John's blurred narrative perspective. Indeed some interpreters hold that the Baptist's words stop with verse 30 and that the rest are the Evangelist's comments; others think that the quotation of the Baptist's words continues through verse 36. Whatever answer one may wish to give to this question, it is not really important. All witnesses have the same mission, the same truth to testify to, and the message carries more weight than its bearer.

The Samaritan Woman and the New Worship

The Samaritan woman is the second character who speaks with Jesus in this section. As a woman and as a representative of the people of Samaria, who because of an age-old feud oppose the Jews, she differs greatly from Nicodemus. The circumstances of her meeting with Jesus differ too; it occurs in the full light of day, the initiative for it lies with Jesus, and it leads to the woman's belief in him and her testimony to her fellow citizens. One has the impression that John, who is the only one to report this episode, has created a diptych, the panels of which, devoted to Nicodemus and the Samaritan, depict the same theme in a different tonality.

The story begins with a twofold transgression. By entering upon a conversation with a woman, and a Samaritan at that, Jesus breaks two taboos. He ignores the partition dividing the two peoples and he disregards the tradition according to which a rabbi should avoid contact with women. Both transgressions are explicitly referred to in the text. The woman voices her surprise that he, a Jew, asks a drink of her, a Samaritan (4:9); and the disciples 'marvelled that he was talking with a woman' (4:27). But whereas the passage tackles the first problem at some length, it does not come to grips with the problem of the relation between man and woman. Indeed, any move in that direction is effectively blocked by the surprising statement in the same verse that 'none said, "What do you wish?" or "Why are you talking with her?" ' One wonders why. There was, as far as one can see, no need for John to refer to the taboo if he was not going to discuss Jesus' attitude to it; and yet mention it he does. In so doing, his text gives rise to an expectation which is, however, immediately stifled. Did John feel that to discuss the

questions that arose in the disciples would be disrespectful
to the Lord? Is this refusal on a par with his desire that Jesus
should be seen to be acting on his own initiative, and does
he simply suggest that there is no more need for Jesus to
justify his conduct than there is for him to be prompted by
others? In such a reading both the transgression of the taboo
and the refusal to account for its transgression would underline the Lord's greatness. One can, however, also refer to the
cultural situation at the time, when questions pertaining to
the relation between man and woman seemed to hold less
interest than they do for us. And yet, the writer of the letter
to the Galatians found it worthwhile to assert that in Christ
'there is neither male nor female' (3:28); one can imagine John
doing the same at this moment of his story, but he does not,
thus leaving us with a question for which we would like to
have an answer.

Not only does Jesus take the initiative for the conversation,
he also inverts the roles. By asking water of the Samaritan, he
puts himself in the dependent position (as he is to do at the
Last Supper?) and yet it is he, not she, who will be the giver
of water and life. But he keeps control over the conversation
itself; he guides it towards the solemn declaration in verse 26:
'I am, the one who is talking to you.' The formula is reminiscent of the Baptist's words and, like them, of God's words
of self-revelation when he speaks to Moses from inside the
burning bush. Its use suggests that Jesus lays claim to being
God or God's equal.

The conversation consists of two sets of three exchanges,
each of which is an utterance of Jesus followed by the
woman's reaction (4:7–9, 10–12, 13–15; 4:16–17a, 17b–19,
21–25) and leading up to the seventh utterance in verse 26,
the words of Jesus just mentioned. His strategy is always the
same. In the first group of exchanges (4:7–15), Jesus uses
the word 'water' in the figurative sense. She thinks he is
talking about the element, whereas he is actually talking about
a different reality, an inner principle of life and fertility, the
symbol of which can be water. One cannot but think of
the waters of the new birth in baptism and the references to
it in the conversation with Nicodemus. In the second group

of three exchanges (4:16–25) the key-word is 'husband'. The woman obviously thinks Jesus means her partner, but he seems to refer to the religious situation of the Samaritans who 'worship what [they] ... do not know' (4:22). They were believed to be the descendants of the people of five towns who had been deported to Palestina and 'worshipped Jahweh but served their own gods' (for the full story, see 2 Kings, chapter 17). In a religious way of looking at things, they had no God: a situation which could be well rendered by the well-known metaphors describing the relation between God and his people as a marriage, and any unfaithfulness on their part as adultery.

The woman's reaction shows that she understands Jesus' way of thinking. In the beginning she does not even call him 'Sir' but simply addresses him as 'you'; in verse 11 she manages to call him 'Sir', but after one further exchange she feels she has to recognize him as a prophet (verse 19). Not surprisingly, she now asks a religious question about the true worship. Jesus' answer about the new worship is consonant with what was said earlier about the new temple. Jesus is the Messiah and more than that. The last utterance in this conversation is the climax in Jesus' self-revelation.

The woman's reaction is appropriate. Words fail her, she leaves her pitcher behind (symbolically?) and invites her fellow-citizens 'to come and see' (4:29). The formula she uses, is familiar; it is the one used by Jesus and later by his disciples to call people to him. For the Samaritans she fulfils the role the disciples had played for each other; she brings the people to Jesus and one can therefore surmise that she has, in contrast with Nicodemus, accepted the message. But she disappears from our sight, and makes room for Jesus; seeing and hearing him, rather than hearing her testimony, makes the Samaritans believe in him (see 4:39–42). But the fact remains that she, a woman and a Samaritan, belongs to the disciples because of her faith and her testimony. If we leave out the apostles, she is, after Mary at Cana, the first genuine believer. She has become what Nicodemus, master in Israel, fails to become.

One more point ought to be made in connection with this dialogue. It begins with Jesus asking for water and it ends with the solemn 'I am ... '. The distance between the two utterances is immense. For this Gospel's statement that Jesus was 'wearied with his journey' (4:6) is unique; nowhere else is his tiredness or weariness mentioned. Moreover, the demand for water is also unique in its genre. I know only one other instance where Jesus demands something for himself, and that is on the cross where he cries out, 'I thirst' (19:28). As these rare utterances point out Jesus' humanity, and as the conversation between Jesus and the woman is so skillfully geared towards the recognition of his godhead, it is tempting to see in its development the passage from a purely human view on Jesus (he is tired, a Jew, thirsty) to the view of faith (he is God's equal). The two terms of the Prologue ('flesh' and 'Word') are here brought together; it is in the flesh that the Word reveals itself. That is not, however, a matter of seeing only, even if the Gospel has so far suggested as much by its insistence on the word 'see'; but here, in the Samaritans' words, it is 'hearing him' (see 4:42) that has converted them. The word you hear is more revealing than the flesh you can see.

One can imagine the problems raised for the first Judaeo-Christian communities by the conversion of Samaritans and similar heretics. The end of this passage (4:31–8) seems to have been written especially with the aim of assuaging doubts and uncertainties about these matters. Jesus' answer to the disciples, who would like to see him eat something, mentions his real food: doing the will of the Father. His attitude to the Samaritans corresponds to God's will; and they are the harvest which the disciples will reap. Once again, there is a certain blurring of the perspective: does what Jesus says in verse 38 and which seems to indicate that the apostles have already been sent, find its right place here, roughly at the beginning of Jesus' public life? Or is it better to read it as a post-paschal utterance which can typify the situation of any disciple at any time?

The Healing of the Official's Son: the New Life

The last passage in this section introduces a third person: the gentile official. Like Nicodemus and the Samaritan, he represents one of the main groups in the Palestinian society of Jesus' days. In them Jesus has met the representatives of his countrymen. However, there is no real conversation between Jesus and the official as there was with the other two. Now his word has a different function. It used to be kerygmatic, the annunciation of the new life in Christ; it seemed subservient to the communication of the message, and to point the way to Jesus and his mission. Here it is different, a power in its own right, healing. The boy who is lying ill in far-away Capernaum, is saved from death by the words Jesus utters in Cana. The text, brief though it is, nevertheless repeats these words three times; 'Your son will live' is said by Jesus (4:50), repeated by the servants (4:51) and quoted by the official (4:53). If one looks back, from this insight, at the words of Jesus in earlier passages, one notices that they already revealed their power of salvation. In the temple episode, Jesus' words spoken at the beginning of his public life will enlighten the disciples after Jesus' death (see 2:22). The Baptist rejoices 'greatly at the bridegroom's voice' (3:29) who 'utters the words of God' (3:34); the Samaritans believe in Jesus 'because of his word' (4:41), and he ends the conversation with the Samaritan with the climactic words: 'I am, the one who is speaking to you.' (4:26). The word, then, is as powerful as Jesus himself. The first sign, at Cana, showed he was the new bridegroom; this second sign, also at Cana, shows the life-giving power of his words. If seeing him is necessary, hearing him is equally important. Because the episode with the official's son manifests that power of Jesus' word, it is called the second sign.

There is a certain vagueness in the text as to this second sign. Is it the second sign at Cana, as verse 5 in chapter 4 seems to suggest, or is it the second sign after his return to Galilee, or is it the second sign absolutely? From other verses in the Gospel we can infer that more signs have been done. Nicodemus mentions the 'signs Jesus does' (3:2), the evangelist speaks of the many in Jerusalem 'who saw the signs which he did' (2:23) and he also mentions that the Galileans had seen 'all that he had done in Jerusalem' (4:45). It would seem, then, that John uses the term, now in a broad sense, referring to several actions of Jesus, and then in a restricted sense, limited to the five or six specific actions which constitute the backbone of his Gospel. Perhaps John's hesitation between a thematic and a historical approach to Jesus (for a discussion of this see Appendix 1) may help to clarify this problem. (In a thematic approach the theme is given right away and then shown again and again; in a historical approach, however, the theme is gradually developed and it acquires new aspects at each turn of the story.) The evangelist's starting-point, which is his belief that the Word has become flesh, leaves open the choice between two ways. The term 'flesh' calls up visibility, the term 'word' is associated with hearing. The difference between the two forms of perception is well known: seeing belongs to space and can perceive at a single glance; hearing is a temporal matter and takes place in succession. In the case of Jesus' self-revelation this means that he can show himself in a moment of seeing, but that his message will require a development in time. Depending on the option taken, the Gospel will focus attention on the visible, the humanity in which the Word becomes manifest, or on the auditive, the communication of the message. This twofold manifestation is already present in the Prologue: 'we have beheld his glory' (1:14) and he declared (*exègèsato*) God' (1:18).

One might want to argue that the word 'sign' in its restricted sense is reserved for the actions where seeing predominates. That would indeed be correct as far as the two episodes at Cana are concerned, even if one has to concede that the visibility of the healing in far-away Capernaum is nil for the people at Cana. Moreover, there are other episodes that are not called signs but which nevertheless have all the characteristics constitutive of the sign in its restricted sense. One thinks here of the cleansing of the Temple, or even of the episode with the Samaritans. The confusion is understandable. Indeed, now that the Word has become flesh, the flesh has become a message that requires reading, and the Word has become visible. The Word become flesh is the flesh become Word. The two mutually exclusive terms 'flesh' and 'word', which are as far apart as 'earth' and 'heaven', have been fused so that the message has all the concreteness of the flesh and the flesh has acquired the meaningfulness of the message. Both must be read, that is interpreted. In the episodes of the first week the stress lay on 'seeing'; here, in the second episode, 'hearing' becomes more important. Jesus' words explain that he is the new temple, and that he invites man to a new life in 'spirit and truth'; the healing of the official's son is the sign of his ability to give that new life. If one looks at the terms 'seeing' and 'hearing' from the disciples' point of view, the two aspects of belief in Christ become manifest: 'seeing' refers to the insight Jesus brings, 'hearing' refers to the new way of life to which they are invited. Belief in Christ is both a view on life and a way of life.

THE THIRD SIGN: WORD OF RECONCILIATION
(Chapter 5)

This rather short section, which coincides with chapter 5, consists of the story of the healing of the cripple and of Jesus' apologia in reply to the Jewish criticism of his behaviour. Unlike the two former signs, the healing is not explicitly named as a sign. But in the following section of the Gospel references are made to the signs Jesus did in Jerusalem; and the present healing is apparently one of them. Moreover, it brings to the fore a hitherto unmentioned aspect of Jesus' being. The new life he brings includes the forgiveness of sins; and of that forgiveness the healed cripple is a sign.

The Healing of the Cripple

The story has an explicitly religious context: it takes place on the Sabbath, at a pool which is believed to be the theatre, now and then, of a divine intervention in favour of one of the many invalids who keep waiting somewhat listlessly for

28

the healing event to happen to them. After the two preceding sections, with their insistence on the newness Jesus brings, one is not surprised to see Jesus replace the old manifestation of God's mercy by a new form of divine presence. The cripple, who belongs to the old world, does not expect anything of Jesus; he is fascinated by the water, looking for the descent of the angel of the Lord; and he seems to have resigned himself to the fact that he will always be late. When Jesus asks him whether he wants to be healed, the man does not express an eagerness to be helped, but he complains about his difficulty in finding one to put him into the water. For him, imprisoned in his old notions, Jesus does not exist. But when Jesus orders him to get up, he is clearly willing to break the rule of the Sabbath. Having waited in the old dispensation for thirty-eight years without any tangible result, the cripple seems willing enough to accept help from elsewhere. Yet, he 'did not know him' (5:13), and he shows a striking lack of interest in the question of who healed him.

At his second meeting with the cripple, Jesus once more takes the lead. Rather than wait for a question from this curiously passive man, he addresses him with the words, 'Sin no more, that nothing worse befall you' (5:14). These words throw a light on Jesus' purpose in healing. What seemed a gratuitous intervention, now proves to be aimed at the man's total renewal. The cripple was healed in order that he might start a new life. The therapeutic action is, therefore, the sign of the forgiveness of sins which is given graciously and which enables man once again to serve the Lord. That is a most appropriate sign, as the cripple who has recovered the use of his legs, can now once again 'walk' or 'follow the paths of God', to use the frequent biblical metaphor for a way of life in obedience to God's commands. By giving the cripple the power to walk by himself, Jesus has created the condition for his renewed service. His word offers forgiveness and reconciliation.

But the man is far from grateful. As soon as he knows who healed him, he goes and tells the Jews. He may be innocent of any guilty motive, but the juxtaposition of Jesus' injunction and the cripple's information of the Jews almost compels the reader to establish a causal link between the two sentences. That such a link can be laid, may be inferred from the fact that, unlike the Samaritan woman, the cripple does not have even an inkling as to who Jesus might be. It is as if he has been healed in vain, for he fails to recognize God's Chosen One. Earlier sayings about the close relation between faith and morality (see, for instance, 3:19–21) point in the same direction; Jesus' words, 'sin no more', may well have wounded him in his self-esteem and thus prevented him from coming to the light. Moreover, there is the terrible saying at the end of chapter 2: 'Jesus did not trust himself to them ... for he himself knew what was in man' (2:24–5). Might not the cripple's reaction be an instance of this truth? Verse 20, 'For every one who does evil, hates the light and does not come to the light', seems a pointed comment on the case.

However, it is dangerous to indulge in psychological hypotheses. The persons Jesus meets are often to be considered as the representatives of a group. That was the case for Nicodemus and the Samaritan woman. The cripple may well be the spokesman of the Jews who rejected Jesus. It is, at any rate, significant that the first great controversy with the Jews should find its origin here in the healing on the Sabbath, and that one of its major themes is 'judgement'.

Jesus' Self-defence

The long discourse, in which Jesus justifies his conduct, has some remarkable formal characteristics. In some parts the first person is used (as in vv.17, 24, 25a, 30–47) whereas the rest (vv.19–23, 25b–29) is written in the third person. In the former Jesus is speaking, in the latter somebody else is speaking about Jesus, or Jesus is speaking about himself as if he were a third person. Even if the two groups were discussing the same themes, the formal differences would differentiate their meaning. For a first-person statement, however objective we try to make it sound, is always linked with the speaker's emotions, whereas a statement in the third person turns the subject under discussion into an object of judgement and appraisal. That shows in the present text. If one reads the I-statements only, one hears a living person passionately upbraiding the Jews for their refusal to accept him. Passion runs high: 'You do not hear his voice'; 'You do not see him'; 'His words are not in your hearts'; 'You do not believe'; 'You think' and so on. But in the other passages one hears a different sound, a voice of cool contemplation, stating facts and thoughts with the objectivity of the doctrinal definition: 'For the Father loves the Son'; 'The Father judges no one'; 'For as the Father has life in himself'. The first series plunges its roots into Jesus' living experience; the second is the result of a theological reflection, or an interpretation of words and deeds in the light of concepts borrowed from elsewhere. Yet the text itself does not make the distinction explicit. It attributes both series to Jesus; and that has to be explained by John's theological starting-point. The Jesus whom the narrator discusses, is at the same time the historical Jesus and the Risen Christ. No distinction is made between them. As a result, words that belong to the post-paschal tradition can be uttered by the historical Jesus.

To quote but one example: to the Son who is to die on the cross, the Father 'has granted . . . also to have life in himself and has given him authority to execute judgement' (5:26–7). Obviously, words such as these have a different meaning when they are spoken before or after the Resurrection; but John does not take that difference into account. Moreover, as the disciples believe in the Risen Christ, their statements about the historical Jesus can be conflated with statements about the Risen Lord; and then it no longer matters who utters a thought, Jesus, the Christ, his disciples or the evangelist, as they all say the same thing. In the present case, all the statements are attributed to Jesus.

There remains another important difference between the two series, and that is to be found in the titles conferred on Jesus. In the 'I-series' Jesus does not define himself, at least not directly. He calls God his Father (5:17), the 'Father who sent me' (5:37), and in this way he implies that he himself is the 'son', but he never uses the term. In the 'he-statements' theological concepts are freely used. Jesus is spoken of as the Son (*passim*), and the term is further defined in two ways, sometimes as 'Son of God', which repeats the metaphor in the conversation with Nicodemus (3:16–19), and sometimes as 'Son of man', another term from the same Nicodemus episode. So far, 'Son of man' has been used three times in this Gospel; once with Nathaniel ('You will see the heavens opened, and the angels of God ascending and descending upon the Son of man' 1:51), once in a reference to the Passion ('the Son of man must be lifted up' (3:14), and here in connection with the judgement entrusted to the 'Son of man' (see 5:26ff.). Is this term to be used especially when Jesus' function in human history is the main focus, and must 'Son of God' be reserved for the special relationship between the Father and Jesus? It is a hypothesis that will have to be tested. Addressing God as 'Father' calls up the correlative term 'son'; via the qualifications 'beloved son', 'only-begotten son', this leads to the absolute statement 'Son of God'. The term 'son of man' does not of itself have a religious connotation; but it was sometimes used in prophetical texts as a form of address, and it was common in the apocalyptic literature of the day as a name for the messianic Saviour. The two terms can have the same referent (as in 5:25 and 27), but they are not synonyms.

If we take the he–statements, with their by now familiar use of repetition and antithesis, we get the following message: Father and Son do the same thing (v.19); the Father loves the Son and shows him everything (v.20); the Father raises the dead and gives them life, the Son also gives life (v.21); the Father judges no one, but the Son judges (v.22); the Father has life in himself and so has the Son (v.26); the Son has received authority to execute judgement (v.27). The notion of judgement, which this text introduces, calls attention to man's attitude and its evaluation: 'He who does not honour the Son does not honour the Father' (v.23); the believer has eternal life and 'does not come into judgement' (v.24). These sentences, in the simple present, have a timeless quality about them; they are a-historical, in the way doctrinal definitions are. What they stress is the unity between the Father and Jesus, and Jesus' authority over man.

In this text these statements serve as background for the

historical conflict between Jesus and the Jews. They explain, or develop, arguments for Jesus' self-defence. Jesus justifies his attitude by claiming equality with God (v.18). In order to strengthen his claim, he appeals to what other witnesses have said about him; the term 'testimony' occurs more than ten times in this short passage. Three instances of testimony are adduced to legitimate Jesus' behaviour: the Baptist who was himself a burning light (vv.33–6); Scripture or its author, Moses (vv.39 and 36); and the works Jesus does which are the outward sign of the Father's testimony (vv.36–7). The Jews' refusal to recognize Jesus is not only a rejection of the words of persons they claim to venerate, it is also a rejection of God himself. In this Gospel, which speaks about the acceptance of Jesus in terms of hearing and seeing, the Jewish position is imputed to the fact that they have never heard God's voice nor seen his form (v.38). This judgement is valid for the Old Testament, but it also bears on the present situation, as in Jesus God manifests himself for all to see and to hear.

What the text says about Moses is puzzling. In verse 46 the letters of Moses (*gramma*) are contrasted with the words (*rhèma*) of Jesus. Jesus' question, 'If you do not believe his writings, how will you believe my words?', can be read in many ways. In one reading the Jews who have not given credence to the written word of Moses are not likely to believe in spoken words; that would imply that the written word of Moses has greater authority for them than the words of Jesus, and yet they refuse their testimony. In another reading this means that the literal message of Scripture, which also points at Jesus as the Messiah, is easier to accept than the words of Jesus with their spiritual meaning; and yet, here too, the Jews have failed to recognize Christ. The words of Jesus, which have not yet been put down in writing, require a spiritual reading; that was manifest in his use of the words 'temple', 'water' and 'birth'. In the second reading offered here that is also true of the Scriptures; they can only function as they should when they are read spiritually. Jesus reads the letter in a new fashion, and thus he is at the same time the fulfilment of Scripture and its transformation.

So far three signs have revealed Jesus to the world. He has been entrusted with a mission which continues his Father's work. He manifests himself as the true bridegroom who will bring about the marriage between God and his people. He will introduce a new form of worship, no longer based on the Temple, and also a new way of reading Scripture in a spiritual sense. For man to enter that new world, he must be born anew and be granted forgiveness. The new (way of) life is offered to all, to Samaritans and Gentiles as well as to the Jews. That too is part of the promise of a new world. But the old world fights back. Having reached this stage the reader is inclined to expect a further development of the message and a growing conflict between Jesus and the Jews. Further reading will confirm this hypothesis.

THE FOURTH SIGN: THE WORD AS BREAD
(Chapter 6)

This section consists of two parts: the first part (6:1–21) covers the events of one day, including the multiplication of the loaves and Jesus walking on the sea; the second part (6:22–71) reports the discussions on the meaning of the bread and the ensuing decisions for or against Jesus. The section concludes with Peter's solemn confession of faith: 'You have the words of eternal life; and we have believed and have come to know that you are the Holy One of God' (6:69).

Bread for the Multitude

The multiplication of the loaves, which is explicitly called 'a sign' (6:14), is also mentioned in the Synoptics. The core of the story – the feeding of the five thousand with an exceedingly small number of loaves – is the same in the four Gospels. But a comparison shows that John differs from the Synoptics (at least for the first multiplication – see Matthew 14, Mark 6 and Luke 9) on four points. First, in the Synoptics the disciples raise the question about the feeding of the crowd, whereas in John it is Jesus who takes the initiative. Second, in the Synoptics Jesus breaks the bread and gives it to the disciples for further distribution (see 'He broke the loaves and gave them to the disciples to distribute', in Mark 6:41); in John, however, 'Jesus took the loaves, and when he had given thanks, he distributed them to those who were seated' (6:11); the text does not mention that he asked the help of his disciples, but suggests he did it all by himself. Third, the traditional formula, 'he took the bread, said the blessing, broke it and gave it,' with its four stages (taking, blessing, breaking, giving), is changed by John into a formula of three stages leaving out the breaking, as can be seen in the quotation above. Fourth, whereas the four Gospels mention that the fragments were gathered, it is only John who writes that this was done at Jesus' command: 'Gather up the fragments left over, that nothing may be lost' (6:12).

If John has introduced these changes, he probably wanted to give the story a special slant, in conformity with his theological views. That is the hypothesis on which this reading rests. Like his predecessors, John writes about the event in relation to the past and to the future. It takes place when 'the Passover, the feast of the Jews, was at hand' (6:4). That inevitably calls up the memory of the trek through the desert and God's gift of the manna, of which this miraculous food seems to be an echo. Not surprisingly, the discussion on its meaning will refer to the manna and to Moses. But next to this reference to the past there is also a reference to what will characterize the first Christian communities – namely, the practice of the Eucharist. Indeed, the formula Jesus uses calls to mind the formula that is used, according to the Synoptics, at the Last Supper and, according to Paul, at each Eucharist in the community. (See, for example, 'during supper he took bread, and having said the blessing he broke it and gave it to them, with the words, "Take this; this is my body" ' (Mark 14:22); or, in the words of Paul in 1 Corinthians 11:17ff., where he comments on their way of eating the Lord's Supper.) Obviously, this is no mere bread. Like the water in the dialogue with the Samaritan woman, or the birth in the conversation with Nicodemus, this is a sign and, as such, it points at something else. But it can also be misunderstood.

That is what actually happens. The jubilant crowd wants to make Jesus king, for the obvious reason that they expect the miracle to become a daily occurrence. Jesus refuses (6:14–16). But the interpretation by the disciples is no more enlightened. They do not see that Jesus, in feeding the crowd, does exactly what God had done for the Jews in their passage through the desert; nor do they understand that, in so doing, he justifies his earlier assertion that he is working just like his Father is. Had they understood that he is God's equal (see 5:18), they would now be less surprised to see Jesus walking towards them on the water (6:19), for that is indeed a divine prerogative as the Old Testament shows. The passage relating this event seems to be out of place here.

The argument that John is only following his sources is neither here nor there, for in his work he obviously arranges and rearranges the material at his disposal according to the requirements of his theology. He might have done the same here as well. If he did not, it must be because the passage has a bearing on the episode with the bread. It relates how Jesus left his disciples to go up the mountain and how he sent them ahead; rowing in hard weather, they see Jesus coming towards them over the water. The setting reminds one of the situation after Easter, when the Lord has ascended to his Father and the disciples feel they are left to fend for themselves. What they are made to discover is that, despite appearances to the contrary, the Lord is with them, the sign of his presence being precisely the Eucharist. If this is correct, the passage shows that the disciples have not yet understood the meaning of the bread, and at the same time it suggests the direction in which one ought to look for an answer. This answer will be provided at length in the following discussion.

The Bread of Life

That this section of the Gospel is linked with the episode of the bread is indicated by its situation in time ('the next morning', 6:22) and by the explicit reference to the bread ('where they ate the bread after the Lord had given thanks', 6:23). Just as at Cana, the unusual, sensational character of the event is underplayed; there is no mention, in the quotation above, of the multiplication of the loaves, but only of the blessing Jesus has given them. The term to refer to this blessing is *eucharistèsantos*. That is, of course, significant. Jesus will make a similar point when he tells his audience that they should not 'labour for the food which perishes, but for the food which endures to eternal life' (6:27) or when he states, towards the end of the discussion, that 'it is the spirit that gives life, the flesh is of no avail' (6:63). The bread is not interesting in itself; it is, obviously, a sign, as the long conversation between Jesus and the Jews will show.

The conversation consists of two parts, the first of which takes place in the synagogue at Capernaum (6:25–59), and the second (6:60–71) continues the same topic with the disciples over an unspecified period of time (6:66). The first part is made up of a number of exchanges in which the Jews ask questions and Jesus answers. The starting-point is the comparison with Moses who gave them the manna; what more has Jesus to offer them? Again, the similarity to the conversation with the Samaritan woman is obvious, though there the point of reference was Jacob. In both cases the meaning of the word, be it 'water' or 'bread', changes from the literal to the figurative; and the dialogue culminates in a confession of faith.

The steps in the argument are easy to follow. Each time, a question gives Jesus an opportunity to clarify his doctrine. A first set of questions introduces several themes: 'When did you come here?' (6:25); 'What must we do?' (6:28); 'What gives you more authority than Moses?' (6:30–1). Jesus answers that he is not bringing them food (6:26–7) but a spiritual message about God and their relation to him, that he expects them to believe in him, that is to follow him (6:29). His superiority over Moses manifests itself in the superiority of the bread he brings over the manna Moses gave: his bread is the bread of God and gives life to the world (6:32–3). From that moment onwards the dialogue takes place on a higher level. In answer to the Jews' demand, 'Lord, give us this bread always' (6:34), Jesus says, 'I am the bread of life' (6:35), a statement the meaning and import of which his further sayings will clarify. The metaphor 'I am bread' almost inevitably calls up the metaphorical meaning of 'eating' while 'I' can be replaced by 'my body or my flesh'. The result is the expression 'eat my flesh', in which the term 'eat' means to 'incorporate' something into one's own being. And what can be the meaning of 'flesh'? We remember that the word was first used in the Prologue in the daring phrase, 'Word made flesh'. It did not mean merely the body of Jesus in its pure materiality, but his humanity. It is his progress through time and space, and his communication with others; it is his body, and the history it makes, from his birth to his later death on the cross; it is his life of a fairly small number of years for the salvation of the world. It is typical of John that he uses the more emotional term *sarx* (flesh) whereas Paul and the Synoptic writers use the term *soma* (body) when they quote Jesus' words at the Last Supper. In such a context the reference to Jesus as the 'Son of man' acquires a new depth (see 6:27, 53, 62). Whenever the term was used, it was always in connection with important moments in the life of Jesus. One remembers allusions to his 'lifting up' (3:13–14) and to his coming as a judge (5:27).

As was to be expected in this Gospel, his audience fails to understand him. They stick to the literal interpretation (see, for example, 6:42 and 6:52). But their unbelief goes deeper than a mere terminological misunderstanding. They refuse to accept that Jesus has been given a mission by God. That is why Jesus keeps repeating that he has been sent by the Father, and that his mission consists in giving life to the people the Father gives him. The real problem is not the metaphors of 'flesh' and 'eating', but the essence of Jesus' being and mission. Yet the metaphors seem to make the communication between Jesus and his audience more difficult; one may therefore wonder why these terms should be used. The answer is to be found in the fact that the term 'flesh' with its connotations of mortality, almost spontaneously calls up the image of the cross on which Jesus will give his life, his 'flesh'. Moreover it also calls up the Eucharist, in which the formula 'this is my flesh', used at the Last Supper, is repeated each time. For the reader of the Gospel, the term is therefore filled with a meaning the richness of which must have escaped the audience at the time when there was no Eucharist and the death on the cross had not yet taken place. To take part in the Eucharist is to take part in the life and death of Christ: 'Who eats my flesh and drinks my blood has eternal life, and I will raise him up at the last day' (6:6, 53).

This theological vision can explain the proper characteristics of John's Gospel in his report on the sign of the bread. If the bread is the symbol of Jesus' life and death for the salvation of the world, one can understand why he himself takes the initiative for distributing it, and why he distributes it all by himself (even if that task will later be entrusted to the disciples). The distribution of the bread and the exact way in which it is done can be considered as prophetic gestures, announcing by the symbol what is so soon to happen. In the light of the association with the Eucharist, it becomes obvious why the fragments left over are treated with an almost liturgical respect. The association with the crucifixion is underlined by the similarity between the symbol and the event; in neither is anything broken, neither the legs of the crucified one, nor the bread Jesus distributes.

The Jews were unable to accept this teaching; and so were many disciples. Jesus now addresses the Twelve (incidentally, this is the first mention of such a group and the writer seems to imply that the reader will know who is meant by the term). To the question whether they too want to leave, Peter answers with a confession of faith: 'You have the words of eternal life' (6:68). His words may lack the depth of Thomas' confession at the end of the Gospel, but they are a fitting conclusion of this part of the Gospel which sees the end of Jesus' activities in Galilee. It shows how his self-revelation is met with faith, even if the beauty of the moment is immediately overshadowed by the announcement of Judas' betrayal.

THE FIFTH SIGN: THE WORD AS LIGHT (7:1—10:39)

The Structure of the Text

Chapter 7 begins with the familiar time indication, *meta tauta* (afterwards), which has so far determined the division of the Gospel into smaller units. Here it functions as the beginning of a new section, but one looks in vain for a repetition of this formula which would then indicate the end of the section. Instead there are some time-indications on the basis of the Jewish feast-days. There are three references to the Jewish feast of the Tabernacles: first it is at hand (7:2), then it is about the middle of the feast (7:14) and, finally, mention is made of 'the last day of the feast, the great day' (7:37). At each of these moments, Jesus gets involved in polemical discussions with the Jews. These discussions continue, introduced by a vague 'again' (8:1 and 8:21). They are followed by the episode with the man born blind (chapter 9), but the moment when these events take place is never mentioned with any precision. The most we can say is that they happen between the feast of the Tabernacles (the harvest festival at the end of September) and the feast of the Dedication (the feast of the light, some three months later). During that period Jesus stays in Jerusalem. When at the end of this period he leaves for the country across the Jordan (10:40), that can serve as an indication that a new section is about to begin.

We shall therefore consider Jesus' stay in Jerusalem over three periods: the feast of the Tabernacles (7:1–52), the period afterwards (8:12—9:41), and the feast of the Dedication (10:1–39). As the episode with the adulterous woman (8:1–11) is generally considered as a non-Johannine insert, it will not be discussed here.

Jesus at the Feast of the Tabernacles

The introduction to this section mentions a group of people, the brothers of Jesus, without any further explanation; their existence, the text supposes, is well known to the readers of the Gospel. They are next of kin to Jesus, but their attitude to him is ambiguous. On the one hand, 'they did not believe in him' (7:5), which corroborates Jesus' earlier statement that 'a prophet has no honour in his own country' (4:44). But, on the other hand, they insist that he should go to Jerusalem to show himself to his disciples and to the world (7:3–4). This contradiction shows that they actually challenge him to go to Jerusalem, probably in the hope that he will fail there, which will put an end to his grandiose claims. As so often in this Gospel, the enemies of Jesus are shown to be both right and wrong. Jesus will indeed go to Jerusalem, but not at their behest, as his hour has not yet come (7:8); he will indeed show himself there, but the failure which his brothers expected, or even hoped for, will turn out to be his triumph.

The attitude of the brothers is not the only problem in this passage. Two sentences claim our special attention. In verse 3 he is told to leave Galilee and to go to Judea 'that the disciples may see the works' he is doing. But that contradicts what was said earlier. The disciples have seen his works, perhaps not all of them but at least a fair number, both in Galilee (Cana, the official's son, the multiplication of the loaves) and in Judea (the cripple). When the brothers repeat their challenge and add, 'show yourself to the world' (7:4), Jesus answers that his hour has not yet come (7:6). And indeed, he will show himself, on the cross, but that does not change the fact that, according to this very Gospel, he has already manifested his glory. If both the disciples and the world are to await a further revelation, the question arises to whom he has so far revealed himself. Or are they to expect a more complete or a more compelling revelation? It would seem that there is always both disclosure and concealment.

The reader may have thought that Jesus had revealed himself in the signs he showed his disciples, but now he is confronted with the promise of a new form of revelation when the time for it, the *kairos*, has come (7:6); that will be discussed later in this chapter. In the mean time Jesus is both hidden and revealed, visible and invisible. Does this duality perhaps account for the startling contrast between his going up to Jerusalem 'not publicly, but in private' (7:10) and his openly teaching in the Temple (7:14)?

This tension between revelation and concealment defines the theme of his life in Jerusalem. Jesus repeats, sometimes verbatim, what he had said before: he comes from God and he has received a mission (for instance, 7:16ff., 7:28–9); he is soon going back to the Father (7:33); because he is one with the Father, he does what the Father does (7:16; 8:28); he brings life to man, and he is the light of the world (8:12). As was announced in the Prologue, this light is not accepted by the darkness; the Jews refuse or fail to see him as what he really is. Their questions and objections show that they do not understand him and that his words veil rather than reveal him. A few examples will do: 'How is it that this man has learning?' (7:15); how can he be the Messiah since we know 'where this man comes from' (7:27); 'What does he mean by saying ... where I am you cannot come?' (7:36). Not only do they misunderstand him, they also oppose him and threaten to imprison him, perhaps even to kill him (7:19 and 23). His words and the signs he does are intended to reveal him and his mission, and yet they have a negative effect; the more he tries to reveal himself, the more he is actually concealed from them.

In these circumstances the conflict is bound to break out. It is painted in the darkest possible colours, as the conflict between two antagonistic principles of light and darkness or as the gap between the world above and the world below; as such it seems inevitable. But at the same time, the evangelist imputes the blame for their failure to receive Christ to the Jews in so far as he establishes a correlation between moral rectitude and faith in Christ. If the Jews had been morally irreprehensible, they would have recognized Christ for what he is and they would have avoided the conflict; but they are not so. Jesus accuses them of judging by appearances (7:24) or according to the flesh (8:15), and he censures them because they 'cannot bear to hear' (8:43) his word. They are thus made responsible for a rejection of Jesus which, in a slightly different light, was fated to happen anyway as light and dark cannot be reconciled, or as the gap between above and below cannot be bridged.

That double vision, which makes the Jews responsible for

the inevitable, turns this section into one of the harshest in the whole New Testament. One can easily understand why. For John, the true believer, it was always a mystery why the Jewish nation, or at least its leaders and a large part of the people, had not received Christ as the Messiah. He can only lay the blame at their door; and yet, at the same time, he seems convinced of the inevitability of the conflict.

This double focus can be found in these chapters. At first, there is a mere distance between Jesus and his opponents: 'Where I am you cannot come' (7:34). They have different value systems: 'You judge according to the flesh' (8:15). They lack insight: 'You know neither me nor my Father' (8:19). Worse still, 'You are from below, I am not of this world' (8:23). Jesus speaks of what he has seen with his Father, but they do what they 'have heard from their father' (8:38), and that is the devil, who is 'a murderer from the beginning, and has nothing to do with the truth' (8:44). When Jesus then reiterates the 'I am' (8:58), which once more expresses his claim to be God's equal, it is not at all surprising that the sons of the devil 'took up stones to throw at him' (8:59). The Son of God is confronted with the arch-enemy.

Yet, Jesus has also manifested his surprise at the unbelief of the Jews. The question, 'Why do you not understand what I say?' (8:43) betrays his, or rather John's, impatience but also shows a genuine incomprehension of their antagonism. The gap between Jesus and the Jews shows beautifully in a discussion about the witness to Jesus (8:13–19). In an earlier controversy on the same subject Jesus is made to say: 'If I bear witness to myself, my testimony is not true' (5:31). Here, some pages later, he states exactly the opposite: 'Even if I do bear witness to myself, my testimony is true' (8:14). The contradiction is so blatant that John must have noticed it. Or was there no contradiction in his eyes? In the speech including the first quotation, Jesus adds that he does not need another witness, but he refers to the Baptist 'that you may be saved' (5:34). There he is willing to meet the Jews halfway, and he agrees that the testimony of one is not valid (see 8:13).

In the new context of chapter 8 he argues that he comes from the Father and goes back to him, which explains why he can dispense with the testimony of man. That seems a vicious circle: it supposes that the Jews will believe his assertion that he is the Son of God on the basis of his being the Son of God. But that is precisely the problem. John, writing his Gospel, need not prove that Jesus is the Son of God. But that belief, which reached its full development after Easter, cannot be present in the hearts and minds of the Jews who see Jesus when his divinity has still to be discovered. Here, once again, are two narrative perspectives, the one looking at Jesus with the veiled eyes of his contemporaries, the other perceiving him with the clear eyes of faith. In the former situation the testimony of others is required, in the latter this is no longer so. But to apply what goes for the later situation to the earlier one is to load the dice against the Jews. That only shows how difficult it must have been for John to write adequately about the Lord. Indeed the terms 'Word' and 'flesh', which both apply to the same person, must of necessity lead to contradictory conclusions. It is a sign of John's greatness that he has not tried to mask this tension, but that he has allowed it to surface time and again.

In the discussion opposing Jesus and the Jews, Abraham is mentioned as a point of reference. In earlier situations other great figures from Israel's history were referred to in order to place Jesus; in the conversation with the Samaritan woman it was Jacob, later it was Moses, now it is the patriarch who is generally considered as the father of the faithful. Jesus rejects the claim of the Jews that they are true sons of Abraham (8:39); instead he maintains that he is the real successor of Abraham (see 8:56). In each of these cases Jesus is seen as the fulfilment of the promise; what the great religious leaders managed to do was but an anticipation in a lower key of what he was to achieve. He gives the living water and the living bread, and is indeed incarnation of faith in God. But Jesus does not only fulfil the Jewish tradition, he transcends it, being older than Abraham (8:58). The formula used to assert this is once again 'I am', the pregnant self-definition of God which Jesus has used as his own in each and every controversy. The Jews, who cannot accept these two claims, need new eyes which would enable them to see in Jesus the genuine son of Abraham and the only Son of God. This great controversy thus leads naturally to the episode with the man born blind who will be given his sight. In that passage the dogmatic debate between the Jews and Jesus is replaced by a lively and realistic dispute between the Jews and the blind man; and in this frame-work the healing of the blind man is clearly a sign, or a symbol, as would be said in contemporary language.

If the Jews need new eyes – that is, a transformation of their whole being, in order to 'see' Jesus – it nevertheless also remains true that the revelation of the Son, however clear it may have been for those who followed Jesus, has not yet been completed. The text refers at least twice to a future moment when the revelation will be completed. In the first of these instances, which is a variation on earlier sayings of the same type using the terms 'Son of man' and 'lift up', Jesus predicts that they will recognize his divinity when he will have been lifted up: 'When you have lifted up the Son of man, then you will know that I am (*ego eimi*)' (8:28). In the conversation with Nicodemus this event had already been referred to (3:14); and there it had been linked explicitly with the well-known episode in the desert when Moses had lifted up a brass serpent, the seeing of which cured the victims bitten by serpents. Here the comparison suggests that Jesus will heal the people looking up at him, when he has been lifted up on the cross. In that reading, the moment of the cross will complete the revelation of Christ.

The use of the title 'Son of man' calls to mind similar statements about a future moment when Jesus will perfect his mission. One can think here of sentences like 'this food the Son of man will give you' (6:27; see also 6:51), or of statements announcing the judgement that has been entrusted to the Son of man (see 5:27–9). That they all contain the title 'Son of man' is revealing, because that term is, as we have seen, closely connected with the suffering of Jesus. The lifting up and what it reveals points to the cross. In other texts, however, Jesus returns to the Father in heaven: 'What if you were to see the Son of man ascending where he was before?' (6:62) or a similar statement in the conversation with Nicodemus (see

3:13). In these instances the lifting up indicates the return to the Father. The fact that the same terms, 'lifting up' and 'Son of man', are used for the return to the Father as well as for the crucifixion shows that the two upward movements coincide; the crucifixion is the return to the Father and therefore also the glorification—the completion of the mission. The *kairos*, or the hour of Jesus is Good Friday. As long as that has not taken place, the revelation is not complete.

The second indication that the revelation is not yet complete is to be found in the saying that 'for as yet the Spirit had not been given, because Jesus was not yet glorified' (7:39). The gift of the Spirit, which depends on the glorification of Jesus, is described in terms reminiscent of Jesus' words to the Samaritan woman: 'The water that I shall give him will become in him a spring of water welling up to eternal life' (4:14). In the chapters under discussion, this becomes: 'He who believes in me, as the scripture has said, "out of his heart shall flow rivers of living water"' (7:38). Verses 7:37–8 can be read in two ways, depending on the punctuation. In the version used above, the waters of the spirit flow in abundance from the heart of the believer; in another version, which places the words 'he who believes in' at the end of the previous sentence ('if anyone thirsts let him come to me and drink, the believer in me'), the spirit flows in abundance from the heart of Jesus. The first reading confirms the words of Jesus to the Samaritan woman quoted above; the second reading is justified by the mention of the water flowing from Jesus' side at the crucifixion (19:34). In either case water and the spirit are linked, the former being a symbol of the latter. This throws light on earlier statements about the new life 'born of water and the Spirit' (3:5). Water and Spirit are two distinct realities, but the element water is both the symbol of the Spirit descending upon man in baptism and a metaphor for the life-giving renewing power which the presence of the Spirit instils in the believer in order to make him new.

When John wrote his Gospel both these founding events, the crucifixion and the descent of the Spirit, had already taken place; and John writes from this knowledge. But what he writes about in his Gospel happened earlier; and John is not always able – or willing? – to make the distinction. One is never certain who is speaking, the historical Jesus or the risen Christ; nor does one know with any certainty whether the Jews he portrays are the contemporaries of Jesus or his own contemporaries. By conflating the two readings, he creates a Gospel that is more theological than historical in its outlook and whose characters are types rather than concrete individuals. That is once again apparent in the story of the man born blind.

The Man Born Blind Sees

As with the previous signs, Jesus takes the initiative here. Uninvited, even without telling the blind man what he is going to do, Jesus anoints the man's eyes with the clay made of spittle and dust, and orders him to go and wash in the pool of Siloam. His purpose is clearly expressed in his answer to a question of the disciples: 'that the works of God might be made manifest in him' (9:3). This repeats a familiar theme: Jesus works the works of God (9:4); in his actions God's working becomes visible. That may be indicated symbolically in the manner in which the healing is performed. Why does he use dust, if not to remind the onlookers of the dust God employed in the creation of man? And why water, if not to allude to the living water which the One sent by God will give to all believers?

Jesus adds an important remark: the time is coming when he will no longer be able to work because of the darkness (9:4). One recognizes the opposition 'light-darkness' which played such an important role in the two preceding chapters. Together with Jesus' words at the end of the passage, 'For judgement I came into this world, that those who do not see may see, and that those who see may become blind' (9:39), this remark links the episode with the previous disputes.

The story is thus embedded in the larger context of the conflict between Jesus and the Jews. Because Jesus interprets his actions himself, there is no need to look for other explanations. The reader may think that Jesus is moved by pity. That would be a perfectly acceptable motive and it is sometimes invoked in the Gospels. In this passage, however, there is not the slightest mention of, or even allusion to, such a motive. Or one might, in the light of the prevailing opinion which linked sin and sickness (see the opinion of the Pharisees in 9:34 and the opinion of the disciples as implied by their question in 9:2), interpret the healing as a forgiveness of sins, comparable to the episode with the cripple. But that is explicitly excluded; 'It was not that this man sinned, or his parents, but that the works of God might be made manifest in him' (9:3). Jesus' answer is not a declaration of principle on the link between sin and sickness; it limits itself to the present case, seeing it as an occasion for the manifestation of God's greatness. That this explanation is so insistently offered shows, of course, that the healing has to be considered as a sign, referring to something beyond itself. The text says as much when it quotes the opinion of those who are favourable to Jesus (9:16). Sight will be a symbol for insight in the person of Jesus; and the blind man will become the representative of all believers.

The man was born blind. Sight cannot be given back to him; it is a new possibility, unimaginable, the beginning of a completely new awareness of the world. He has become a new creation, as the reactions of his acquaintances show; they do not recognize him and doubt whether he is the man they used to see (9:8–9). The Pharisees, too, have their doubts, and question his parents. But these are so afraid of the Jews that they prefer not to answer (9:22–6). Anyone who commits himself, in one way or another, to Jesus will, as this man's fate shows, be cast out of the synagogue (9:34), not only at the time of Jesus but also at the time this Gospel was written. It is the Johannine way of presenting Jesus as a sign of contradiction and of predicting the strife that will, as the Synoptics have it, divide families and communities in two groups, those who see Jesus and those who don't.

The blind man sees, after he has been touched by Jesus and after he has fulfilled his part. He has 'heard' the Word and listened to it before he was able to see. Even in his seeing there are degrees. In the beginning he cannot, even though he sees, answer the question where Jesus is. If one remembers the importance of the phrase 'come and see' in the first chapters, one realizes that the question, 'where is he?' (9:12), masks the much more challenging question, 'Who is he?' But later, in his discussions with the Pharisees, he will give evidence of a growing insight; he now declares that Jesus is a prophet (9:17). In a third stage, he confesses his faith in the Son of man (see 9:35–8), thus completing the movement from blindness to insight. Two factors appear to have played a part in this process of discovery. The constant nagging of the Pharisees and the need to formulate for others and for himself what had really happened, may well have made him bear witness, even if he did not especially want to, and that may have speeded up the process of insight. But this is a reading for which there is no evidence in the text apart from the fact that he must indeed repeat again and again what had happened. For the second factor, the text is more explicit. In this Gospel, 'seeing' Jesus himself leads to faith. Others may have spoken about him, but the final commitment is always made when the prospective believer sees, and/or hears, Jesus. Here also that is the case. The man confesses his faith in a direct answer to the words of Jesus: 'You have seen him, and it is he who speaks to you' (9:37).

One more remark must be made in connection with this confession. The first two statements of the blind man about Jesus are factual and referential, and they do not commit the one who utters them to any course of action. The third statement, however, is performative and auto-implicative. It brings about what it states – faith becomes a reality when the speaker confesses it; and it implies a course of action which corresponds to the commitment undertaken. In the present case the man suits the action to the word and 'worships' him (9:38). He is the first to do so in this Gospel. Others have already come to believe in Jesus, but none (apart from the disciples represented by Peter—see 6:67ff.) has expressed his faith in word and action in a direct confession to Jesus. The man does not formulate a doctrinal belief in the person of Jesus; he merely says, 'I believe', which indicates a way of life. This new-born man has entered the new world which Jesus has opened up for him. He becomes a member of the group of believers who share in Jesus' life.

There is a tiny indication of this unity between Jesus and his followers at the beginning of this passage. There Jesus says, 'We must work the works of him who sent me' (9,4). In itself this 'we' is not so important, and in some manuscripts it is indeed replaced by 'I'. But there are similar passages earlier on (see 3:11) where the same substitution can be found. This is a prelude to later discourses of Jesus in which the unity between him and his followers will be described. Here that unity shows, almost unawares. But that is to be explained by the fact, which has often been commented upon, that John writes from the fullness of faith. He may have wanted to show both the progress in Christ's self-revelation and the growth of faith in the disciples, but this plan has been thwarted, at least partly, by the strength of his belief in the risen Christ.

The Good Shepherd

The division in chapters is misleading here; it suggests that the story about the good shepherd belongs to a new section; it does not. There are important new elements, as we shall see presently, but there is no formal or thematical break with the previous chapters. Thematically, the text plays with the notions of 'hearing the voice', of 'knowing' the shepherd and the sheep; and that reminds one of the importance given in the previous passage to knowing Jesus. Formally, the new discourse is introduced without any of the usual signals announcing a new situation, such as 'and Jesus said', or 'cried out', or 'again'. Moreover, this passage ends in verses 19–21 with a description of the diverging reactions of the Jews. As if to underline the link with the previous passage its last words raise the question: 'Could an evil spirit open a blind man's eyes?' We shall then take this into account and treat this passage as a part of the larger whole centring on the fifth sign.

The text itself advances step by step, and it culminates in two metaphors that reveal essential and new aspects of Jesus' being and mission. The first metaphor is that of the door of the sheep's pen (see 10:7); the second metaphor describes Jesus as the 'good shepherd' (10:14). These two metaphors have a twofold function: they help the reader to understand Jesus, but they also serve to characterize Jesus' enemies. These do not enter the pen by the door – that is, in union with Jesus – and they are therefore called thieves and robbers (10:1); as such they are contrasted with the good shepherd, Jesus. Now, in the episode with the man born blind a distinction was made between the people and its leaders. The latter had decided that 'if anyone should confess him to be Christ, he was to be put out of the synagogue' (9:22), and that is indeed what happens to the blind man (9:34). By their actions the leaders attempt to block the way to Christ, but in doing that they keep the people away from the good shepherd who brings safety to his flock and leads them to pasture. Their attitude, which was so severely condemned because it repudiated Jesus, is now seen to be even more condemnable because it is also a crime against the people.

In stark contrast to these hirelings, Jesus is the good shepherd. That term deserves some explanation. In the original Greek, the shepherd is not called *agathos*, which means 'good', but *kalos*, which means 'beautiful'. As it is accepted nowadays, this word 'conveys a closeness to perfection which gives intellectual and/or spiritual satisfaction as well as sensuous pleasure,' says the *Longman Dictionary of the English Language*. So one cannot help wondering why the Greek term has always been translated by 'good', which is now hallowed by usage, and not by 'beautiful' which would have hinted at the fascination Jesus can exert and which manifests itself in works such as the well-known sculpture of 'le beau Dieu' in Amiens. The term 'shepherd' harks back to numerous instances in the Bible where God is leading the flock of Israel or where great leaders, such as David or Moses, are given that same task. It should, moreover, be pointed out that a metaphor with its word-field of 'shepherd', 'flock', 'grazing', 'obedience', etc. offers possibilities for development beyond those of the metaphors 'I am the living water'. The latter are of necessity one-sided, as they do not include the idea of a certain reciprocity which the 'sheep' metaphor does indeed contain.

That idea will dominate Jesus' discourse. In order to explain why he is the good shepherd, Jesus points at the close relationship between him and his disciples: 'I know my own, and my own know me' (10:14). In biblical parlance, the term 'to know' indicates a relationship in which other than mere rational factors play their part. It does not refer to the objective knowledge of, say, a thing; it denotes a relationship involving mutual trust and responsibility, and it is also used for sexual congress. That inter-personal dimension of the term is underscored by the deep affective tonus of the passage which is about more than words. Jesus gives his life, freely, of his own accord. Furthermore, his love of his flock is intimately intertwined with his love of the Father. There is even a parallelism between the love of the Father and the Son on the one hand, and the love of Jesus and his own on the other hand. As the Father knows Jesus and Jesus knows the Father (see 10:15), Jesus knows his own and they know him (see 10:14).

That dimension of the relation between Jesus and his own is a new factor in the Gospel. So far, references have been to belief in Jesus, 'seeing' him and 'hearing' him; or else Jesus has called himself 'the bread' or 'the water'. Now, the 'laying down of his life for the sake of the flock' (10:17–18) introduces an example what can only be called 'love'. The parallelism mentioned above between the relation of Jesus to his Father and the relation of Jesus to his flock brings the idea to the fore for the first time in this Gospel. The term *Agapeô*, a typically Christian term which has so far been seldom used, denotes the love of the Father for the Son or for the world (see 3:16, 3:35, 5:20 where the less distinctive *philein* is used). That always happened in the third person, which is the grammatical person used for conveying information. Here the relation between Jesus and his flock is expressed by Jesus speaking in the first person: 'I know my own ... I lay down my life for the sheep ... I lay it down of my own accord' (10:14–18). That is no mere communication of information;

it functions as a performative utterance creating what it says and inaugurating the future.

Moreover, Jesus appears in this formula as the central figure, the intersection where two movements meet. As the Father knows him, he knows his own; and his own know him as he knows the Father (see 10:14–15). It looks as if the Father's love for human kind, and human knowledge of the Father pass through Jesus. He occupies a key position; he is the intermediary between the world above and the world below, between God and man. That is an exceedingly rich idea, the full meaning of which will probably unfold as our reading of the Gospel continues.

But the idea of love and the place of Jesus in that exchange is not the only new element in this short discourse. There is also a mention of other sheep not belonging to the flock (see 10:16). Is this an allusion to the universal mission of Jesus who has come for all human kind? The theme is lightly touched upon, perhaps as an anticipation of later developments. That aspect, however, is related to the reach of the mission; and that is, at present, less important than our understanding of its aims. What we have discovered so far is this: in the name of the Father, Jesus brings about a new world and a new life, with new food, new water, new worship. It consists in a new relation to God – and by implication to human kind – in which he occupies the central position. This summary is given at the end of the section on the fifth sign, in the final passage, which deals with the feast of the Dedication.

The Feast of the Dedication

Jesus' appearance in the Temple at the feast of the Dedication ends this account of his third stay in Jerusalem. Afterwards he crosses the Jordan and stays there in the place where the Baptist had sojourned (see 10:40). Is this significant or is it pure coincidence? There are no elements in the text which allow us to answer that question satisfactorily.

In the Temple Jesus again proclaims his message. He rejects the Jews who have rejected him, saying that they do not belong to his flock. Those who do, will be given eternal life;

such is indeed the will of the Father; and he and the Father are one (10:30). There follows a strange episode in which Jesus defends himself against the anger of the Jews by having recourse to what must seem a subterfuge. He appeals to the fact that Scripture 'called them gods to whom the word of God came' (10:35); if that was legitimate – and how could a true Jew doubt the testimony of Scripture? – it was no doubt legitimate for Jesus to say, 'I am the Son of God' (10:36). John is so full of respect for Jesus that he would be inconsistent with himself if he reduced this answer to nothing more than a cunning move. It is one indeed, but it also discloses a scene of awe-inspiring depth. The polemical situation gives the evangelist an opportunity to remind his audience of the gift Jesus has brought them. If that gift is really, as he claims, life eternal, and if baptism in the spirit really renews man, then the words of the Old Testament speak the truth about man in a way its great writers did not understand. Man, reborn in Christ, is, in the words of the Prologue, 'born, not of blood nor of the will of the flesh nor of the will of man, but of God' (1:13). The assertion that Jesus is God's Son would, in such a reading, be indissoluble from the assertion that those who believe in him are also children of God. This passage, placed at the feast of the Dedication of the Temple, throws light, not only on the relation between Jesus and his Father, but also on the relation between the Father and the followers of Jesus. One of the Church fathers was later to formulate this in the scintillating aphorism: 'God became man, so that man could become God.'

This is a fitting conclusion to a long section that centres on the man who was born blind and was, as it were, created anew by Jesus. The section reveals that the relation between Father and Son is a relation of love, and that human kind finds its saviour in Jesus. The gift he brings can be described in the terms 'bread, life, water'. But as the revelation unfolds it becomes more and more evident that these are metaphors for another, deeper reality for which the equally metaphorical terms 'spirit, the life of God, children of God' are perhaps most appropriate. The revelation of Jesus as the Son is completed by the revelation of the believers as sons and daughters of God. Jesus is the revelation of God's love, understood as our love of God as much as God's love of us. Jesus stands at the centre of the world and of history, the Son of man who is the Son of God.

THE SIXTH SIGN: THE WORD AS LIFE (10:40—11:56)

The story of Lazarus occurs only in the Gospel of John. Like all good stories it consists of three stages, each is connected with its own locale. The story begins across the Jordan where Jesus has retired after the feast of the Dedication; he receives a message telling him that his friend Lazarus is mortally ill with the implicit demand that he come and save the man from death. In narrative terms this is the phase of the contract. In the second phase, that of the test, the protagonist must show whether he is able to honour the contract; in the Gospel Jesus arrives at Bethany, but he is late and Lazarus has died. In the third phase, Jesus goes to the tomb and raises Lazarus to life; that is the phase of the glorification where the protagonist is recognized by all.

The Death of Lazarus

When Jesus hears the news of Lazarus' mortal illness, he accepts the invitation to come and save his friend, which means that a contract has been tacitly agreed upon. He will come and do what he has been asked to do. Yet, for some unstated reason, he postpones his departure for two days (see 11:6). The reader remembers that this refusal to accede immediately to a demand is typical of Jesus in this Gospel; it happened at Cana, and in all his actions where Jesus keeps the initiative. His 'signs' do not depend on the desire or the demand of others, but only on the will of his Father. He says so here, in very clear terms: 'It is for the glory of God, so that the Son of God may be glorified by means of it' (11:4). The reader knows that the glorification is, in this Gospel, the

55

same as the crucifixion. But he has the benefit of hindsight; the disciples haven't. They need more insight; and that will be given them in a long conversation with Jesus (11:7–16).

At first, they do not want to return to Judea, because they fear the enmity of the Jews (11:8). In a variation on an earlier saying (see 9:4–5) Jesus declares that one must walk as long as it is daylight, the implication being that the night has not yet come. When it comes he will be betrayed, as the evangelist states emphatically (see 13:30). But in the mean time there is no sufficient reason for not going into Judea. However, having said that, Jesus introduces a new element of misunderstanding by calling Lazarus' condition a sleep. True to the pattern of this Gospel, the disciples understand the word literally, whereas Jesus has used it as a metaphor for death (11:11ff.). He knows – how? – that Lazarus is dead, and he is glad for the sake of his disciples that he was not there, 'so that you may believe' (11:15). It is as if he has deliberately waited until Lazarus was dead, so that he would have a chance of showing his mastery over death. As his disciples will so soon be confronted with his death on the cross, a sign revealing that mastery is most welcome. Yet they misunderstand Jesus' words; they believe he is inviting them to come and die with him (11:14–16). The first phase of this narrative thus sets the stage for what is about to happen; it links the Lazarus episode with the death of Jesus himself and also, in a slightly different way, with the fate of the disciples. These events will have to be read in the light of what happens to Lazarus. It is a sign (see 12:28).

The Coming of Jesus

When he is nearing Bethany Jesus is met by the two sisters, first by Martha, then by Mary. The meeting takes place in the same spot, as is explicitly stated (11:30), and they greet him in the same words: 'Lord, if you had been here, my brother would not have died' (11:21 and 32). But now, they imply, it is too late. For them, just as for the onlookers, death is final and irrevocable. Martha's famous 'Now he will smell, for he has been dead for four days' (11:39) graphically expresses this conviction. But they do believe in the resurrection at the last day (11:24). Against the backdrop of this Jewish belief, Jesus' assertion that he is the 'resurrection and the life' (11:25) acquires its full meaning. What he seems to be saying is that the last day has come and that the gift of eternal life has been entrusted to him. Martha's answer to these words is a confession of faith in Jesus; she calls him the Christ, 'the Son of God' (11:27). Apparently she has forgotten her brother; she does not even as much as mention his name. Is that a sign of her trust in Jesus? It is, at any rate, remarkable that she invites her sister to go and see the Lord, without having been told to do so, or without promising that he will intervene. Why does she say that 'the Teacher is calling for her' (11:28), and why does she keep that a secret, as the Greek suggests? Does she want to share her vision of faith with her sister? And with her sister only? We remember from earlier episodes that the true believer brings his friends to Jesus, and that it is the meeting with him that is the basis of faith. Here, in the face of the failure to save Lazarus' life, one of the sisters expresses her faith in Jesus and invites the other to adopt the same attitude. Although the text does not say that Mary believes, we can safely state that her faith too precedes the sign. It is because Martha has seen and heard Jesus that she believes, not because she has seen the raising of her brother. By directing Mary to go and see Jesus in the place where she had met him and expressed her faith, she obviously wants her to share the same experience. What neither she nor her sister expect is that Jesus will call their brother to life again. Their faith does not depend on that event.

Lazarus Raised from the Dead

What happens then, in the third stage, is quite unexpected. Jesus asks to be shown the grave where his friend has been buried, and the whole group follows him there. Martha's reaction quoted before about the irreversibility of death, and the question from the onlookers as to whether Jesus could not 'have kept this man from dying' (11:37) are ample evidence that nobody so much as entertained the idea that the raising of a dead man would happen. Death is the final reality; and one can only weep. Jesus too is deeply moved. In a Gospel which hardly ever refers to Jesus's feelings the threefold mention of his emotions in this situation (11:33, 35, 38) is striking. But the Gospel does not describe the nature of these emotions; it mentions 'weeping' and, according to the literal translation in the RSV Interlinear, 'groaning in himself' (11:35). One can, of course, start surmising and invoke all sorts of psychological explanations: he might be weeping because he feels sympathy with the mourners, or because his friend's death touches him so deeply, or because he is reminded of his own impending death. But one should remember that John never uses psychological motivations; he is more of a theologian who looks for a theological explanation. Jesus' behaviour is – and we have his word for it – motivated by the desire to bring the people to faith in him and in the Father who sent him (11:42). That is a formidable task, and one which proves to be more demanding than was anticipated. In that perspective Jesus might be weeping over Jerusalem for its lack of faith. In one sense, the raising of Lazarus cannot create faith, as faith must precede: 'Did I not tell you that if you would believe you would see the glory of God?' (11:40). But in another sense, the sign is expected to generate faith. As we shall see in a moment, it does and it does not. Even this sign cannot persuade people to believe in Jesus. Is his awareness of this situation the motive for Jesus' weeping?

The raising of Lazarus is entirely Jesus' decision. He cries out with a loud voice (11:43) because, as he had said earlier, 'the dead will hear the voice of the Son' (5:25). His word which made the cripple walk and reached the official's son in spite of the distance, resounds with the creative power of God's word in the simple command, 'Lazarus, come out!' (11:43). And the dead one arises and goes his way, unbound. That nobody asks him about his experiences in the other world or that he does not reveal anything about them, will amaze the contemporary reader of the Gospel, but in the text itself his silence is self-evident. He is not the hero of the story; that is Jesus in whom God's glory has manifested itself. He is the master of life and death.

About the reactions of the bystanders we can be brief. Many believed in him, and a lot of others did not. In their short-sightedness the Pharisees even decide to have the Master of Life killed. But even then, they can only speak God's word. Caiaphas, who thinks it is better 'that one man should die for the nation' (11:49) does not realize he is speaking the truth. The evangelist, in his commentary, calls this statement a prophecy (11:52). That means that Caiaphas is the spokesman of God. He means, of course, that Jesus has to die in order to avoid a political crisis, but in saying that, he also asserts unwittingly the religious truth that Jesus lays down his life for the salvation of the world. The double meaning, which the words of Jesus so often have, is now also to be found in the utterances of his enemies. What they have to say is more than what they want to say. The suggestion is that Caiaphas, like Judas or Pontius Pilate, plays a part in God's plans; and that seems questionable. Perhaps the double narrative perspective sheds light on this problem. When things were about to happen, an action like that of Caiaphas could only be understood as part of a hateful plot against Jesus. Once, however, the story has run its course, the different actors in it can be viewed as serving God's grand design. Then everything falls into place, and what seemed contingent and avoidable proves to have been necessary. That does not entail a deterministic view of human affairs; it does not mean that it had to happen, but that once it happened its function in the story becomes manifest: it had to be that way.

THE LAST WEEK

THE SEVENTH SIGN: THE CROSS

THE STORY OF the last week in Jesus' life takes up the greater part of the Gospel. No less than six chapters are devoted to it; three of them, chapters 15—17, consist almost exclusively of words of Jesus, and the previous three (chapters.12—14) relate words and events. Time-indications are scarce. The Jewish Passover is announced in 11:55; 'six days before the Passover' (12:1) Jesus is at supper with Lazarus, and the 'next day' (12:12) he enters Jerusalem. On an unspecified day before the Passover (13:1) Jesus and the disciples share the Last Supper; the next morning (18:28) he is brought before Pontius Pilate, and eventually condemned to death 'on the day of Preparation of the Passover; it was about the sixth hour' (19:14). He dies the same day and is buried. These time-indications are not used as structuring devices, but they are mentioned occasionally. Moreover, there are no other salient structuring elements; the story unfolds in a straightforward manner. For the sake of clarity it is advisable to divide this long narrative into smaller units. We shall look in succession at the beginning of the week (11:54—12:50), the Last Supper (13:1—17:26), and the Passion and Death (18:1—19:42).

THE BEGINNING OF THE WEEK (Chapter 12)

After the raising of Lazarus, Jesus withdrew to a place called Ephraïm (11:54). Now the Passover is at hand, he comes back

60

to Jerusalem. Three events mark the beginning of this week: Mary's anointing of his feet, his entry into Jerusalem, and the attempts of the Greeks to see him. Thematically, these events are unrelated, but they have structural aspects in common. In the first place, although they place Jesus at the centre of the events, they do not give him the active role. In contrast with other events in the Gospel, he is here shown submitting himself to others: he is anointed, he is welcomed in Jerusalem, he is searched for by the Greeks. Since his baptism, in which he also underwent the action, this is the first time that he is not the subject but the object of action. Moreover, whilst submitting himself, he nevertheless interprets the action and subtly alters its meaning.

The Anointing at Bethany

John's account of the events is puzzling. He mentions Mary's anointing of Jesus as having taken place after the raising of Lazarus (see 12:1), whereas in his account of that event itself the anointing is mentioned as if it had preceded the raising (see 11:2). A comparison with the Synoptics is not very illuminating. There are major differences among them. To mention some: Luke turns the woman into a public sinner and places the event at a much earlier time (Luke 7:36–8); the other two place it at Bethany but in another house, and have an unknown woman anoint the head of Jesus (see Mark 14:3–10 and Matthew 26:6–13). Different hypotheses can be construed to account for these divergencies, but if one considers the link of this passage with the other two dealing with the beginning of the week, a theological motivation presents itself. If John had placed the anointing before the raising, he would have destroyed the beautiful unity of Jesus' sovereign behaviour up to and including the Lazarus episode; and he would not have been able to introduce the Passion, where Jesus undergoes the event, with such conviction. Now the three episodes point to the same end, death; and in making Jesus endure the action, they anticipate the final suffering.

Mary does not explain her action, and rightly not, for it is an excessive, irrational gesture which can, in this context after her brother has been brought back to life, be interpreted as a token of gratitude and wordless worship. Judas Iscariot cannot see it that way; for him it is a waste of money which could have been put to better use in helping the poor. John cannot refrain from blackening Judas and accuses him of avarice; just like earlier remarks about the devil as the father of the Jews, this one shows that he cannot understand how some people do not see the Christ in Jesus (12:4–8). Jesus himself, who patiently undergoes the anointing, gives it a new meaning by relating it to his death. The text of verse 7 is probably corrupt, and it can be read in two ways. Either it means, 'Let her keep it for the day of my burial' (12:7), or, 'She has anticipated the day of my burial'. In either case, the link between burial and anointing is obvious. His words change the meaning of Mary's gesture. What might have been an act of gratitude, the anointing which he endures, becomes a sign of the death he will have to suffer. What was thought of as an act of glorification turns out, in the eyes of Jesus at least, to be a homage to one marked for death. Once again, glorification and humiliation coincide.

The Entry into Jerusalem

In this second passage we meet the same paradox as in the previous one. Jesus is led in triumph into Jerusalem and he puts up with it, even though he knows the fickleness of the people. He is the one about whom it was said ominously that he knew what was in man (see 2:25). He endures the enthusiasm of the crowd, but by choosing an ass's colt to ride on, he alters the meaning of the procession. Anyone who has ever watched an adult ride on a donkey knows that in these circumstances Jesus' behaviour cannot but be seen as a parody of a triumphant war-hero entering his city. That is so true, that John feels the need to justify Jesus' behaviour. After the Resurrection, the disciples will find a justification in an Old Testament text announcing the coming of Sion's king riding an ass's colt (12:14–16). Jesus is thus both glorified and ridiculed, which shows once again the double focus of this text. The dual meaning prefigures the events of the Passion which will have exactly the same twofold meaning. The Scriptures can be applied to Jesus, and that shows that he is their fulfilment, but he also imposes a new meaning on to them, which shows that he transcends them.

Jesus and the Greeks

The third passage in this section introduces a new group, the so-called Greeks, probably converts from the pagan world who have adopted the Jewish religion. They wish to see Jesus (12:21), an expression which, it will be remembered, indicates the wish to know more about him. Exactly as in the first week, the disciples function as intermediaries between the prospective believers and Jesus; Philip tells Andrew, and they tell Jesus (12:22). The apparent irrelevance of this detail raises the question why Jesus has all of a sudden to be approached with such caution. The disciples seem to hesitate before telling Jesus of the request of the Greeks; they must have found this request so strange that they needed the mutual reassurance of the other's presence before telling Jesus. This may have something to do with the accession of non-Jews to the first Christian communities, which was, as is well known, a major problem. For Jesus, however, it is not. He interprets the request as evidence of his glorification (12:23), as it means his recognition by people from afar; but the nearness of his hour is, of course, also the nearness of his death. The very fact that he is there, not only for the Jews but for the Gentiles as well, implies a break with the Jewish tradition which will naturally stir up controversies and conflicts. It is against this background that his further remarks must be seen. They refer both to his own Passion and to the sufferings of his followers.

These remarks have a markedly literary form through their use of parallelism, which reminds one of similar structures in the Prologue. They seem to have the character of a formula, which makes them easy to remember. To take a case in point: after the introductory 'Truly, truly, I say to you' (12:24), which gives weight to what is to follow, three complex sentences describe the situation in strongly symmetrical and/or antithetical structures: 'If [not] . . . dies, it remains alone, but if it dies, it bears fruit; one loving life loses, and one hating life will keep it; if anyone serves me, [he must follow] and where I am he will be; if anyone serves me, the Father will honour him' (12:24–7). This structure points the way towards a reading of the text: the terms 'alone, lose one's life' are to be considered as synonyms; and so are the terms 'bear fruit, keep life, be where Christ is, to be honoured by the Father'. These truths apply to Jesus; hence his being troubled and his prayer (see 12:27). But they also apply to the disciples who serve him. That the Gentiles accept Christ glorifies him and the disciples as well, but it is also an additional source of conflict for them. Because of the close relationship between Jesus and his disciples, glorification is inevitably also accompanied by suffering for them.

For the rest, Jesus repeats truths that are familiar to the reader, but they have to be repeated in order to enter the minds and hearts of his audience. One such repetition is the opposition 'light-darkness' in verses 35–6. There he tells people to walk in the light: 'The *light* is with you ... walk in the *light*; lest the *darkness* overtake ... who walks in *darkness*; while you have the *light* ... believe in the *light* ... sons of *light*'. Another formulaic utterance occurs in verses 44–50. 'He who believes in me ... believes in him who sent me. He who sees me ... sees him who sent me,' is a good example of repetition. The next verses are an instance of a more associative process: 'If anyone does not keep my *words*, I do not *judge* (for I did not come to *judge*, but to save) ... Who rejects my *words*, has a *judge* ... *words* that I have spoken will *judge* ... I did not speak of myself, but the Father commands me what to say and his command ... I say.' It will have become obvious that in these sayings nothing new is brought forward; they are theological statements in a fairly mnemonic form, and they can be inserted at any time into the story as a doctrinal commentary.

That is true also of the passage in which John tries to understand the unbelief of the Jews. He uses a quotation from Isaiah which describes the people's blindness as willed by God (12:38–40); in that perspective the unbelieving Jews appear as helpless victims of God's judgement. Yet, in the same breath John explains that many believed but did not dare to confess it for fear of the authorities (12:42–3); and in that perspective they seem to foil God's aim as they come to an insight which he was supposed to have denied them. The paradox shows, once again, that John is trying to find explanations for the inexplicable.

The main theme of these three passages regarding the last week of Jesus' life is undoubtedly the binomial 'glorification-crucifixion'. So far, each mention of the glorification has implied a reference to suffering; it appears that a reference to the crucifixion will automatically entail a mention of the glorification. In a chiasmic structure the term 'glorification-suffering' would be turned around into 'suffering-glorification'; that is a hypothesis that further reading will verify or disprove.

THURSDAY: THE LAST SUPPER

The section describing the events on Maundy Thursday is a very long one. It begins at 13:1 with the solemn announcement that Jesus' hour has arrived and it ends with the departure of Jesus and his disciples to the garden across the Kidron valley (18:1). That stretch can be divided into two parts: the first one ends with Jesus inviting his disciples to rise and to 'go hence' (14:31); the second one relates one more farewell discourse and a public prayer of Jesus. One has the impression that the evangelist had second thoughts after the first farewell discourse and that he wanted to try again to emphasize what was coming.

Washing of the Feet

The introductory sentences to this first part are unusually solemn, even for John; it is as if they do not belong to a plain narrative, but have been lifted verbatim from a liturgical proclamation. With a baffling self-assurance the evangelist takes it upon himself to describe what goes on in Jesus' mind and how he interprets the events: 'Jesus knew that his hour had come to depart out of this world to the Father, having loved his own who were in the world, he loved them to the end' (13:1). This sentence sets the limits within which the coming events will have to be read. John repeats the strategic movement with which he began his Gospel; he summarizes the main truth and then he shows how this became reality in concrete events and words.

He begins with the washing of the feet. As if to remind the reader that the coming passage must be read in the proper perspective, he repeats once again that Jesus knew that 'the Father had laid all things into his hands, and that he had come from God and was going to God' (13:3). This awareness leads to the prophetic gesture of the washing of the feet. No specific relationship between the two is mentioned, but one has the impression that the visible action ('He rose ... laid aside his garments, and girded himself with a towel', 13:4) is a sign of his inner motivation; his consciousness shows in the laying down of his garments. Such details had a meaning for John and that is why he mentioned them though he could, from a purely narrative point of view, equally well have omitted them. Is this perhaps a sign that Jesus has laid down his greatness and taken on the semblance of a slave? If the expression 'invest someone with authority' uses the idea of dressing as a symbol for conferring authority or glory on someone, the antonymous 'to divest' can be used as a symbol of renunciation or spoliation.

Although Jesus will call his action an example for his disciples, one must not say that he has done it in order to give an example. To reduce his action to such a motive would be to belittle it. The Word has become flesh: that is the basic action and the supreme form of humility which is now carried out in the serving of his disciples and in the laying down of his life for them. He is humble, not because he wishes to look humble, but because he is who he is; and the washing of the feet is but one of the ways in which his being manifests itself.

Washing of feet is not required by any Jewish rule; for one thing, it happens during supper and not before it (13:2) and, moreover, Jesus himself says to his disciples that they are clean (13:10). It is thus an absolutely gratuitous gesture, and as such it is symbolically overdetermined. Informed of its meaning by the opening lines of the passage, the reader is expected to see it as a manifestation of Jesus' love towards his disciples, as the expression of his awareness of the impending Passion, and as the sign of his laying down his life in complete freedom.

Peter does not understand that. As was to be expected in this Gospel, he merely sees the outward aspect of Jesus' behaviour. He refuses to accept that the relation between Jesus and his disciples should be turned upside down; and he is willing to submit only when he hears that unless he does so he will 'have no part' (13:8) in Jesus. He is made to understand that one can only share in the free gift of Jesus' goodness if one accepts his humility and his passion. Apart from this spiritual meaning, the washing of the feet also has a moral dimension: the disciple is told to repeat Jesus' gesture, not only in its material form but in everything that the gesture represents. John formulates this in terms of mission and identity: 'He who receives any one whom I send receives me; and he who receives me receives him who sent me' (13:20). There is a parallelism between the Son sent by the Father, and the disciple sent by the Son; as the Father is seen in the Son, so the Son is seen in the disciple. But that is true only if the disciple acts like Jesus.

Judas' Betrayal

In keeping with the general intention of this Gospel, Jesus is not the helpless victim of Judas' betrayal. Whenever he can, John stresses Jesus' foreknowledge of what is to happen (see 13:11, 18). There is a longer passage (13:21–30) in which the betrayal is openly discussed. It contains a number of puzzling details. What is the meaning of the fact that Peter does not address Jesus but the disciple 'whom Jesus loved' in order to find out who the traitor is? In answer to the beloved disciple's question Jesus does not, it is true, name Judas, but the indication is almost as clear. Yet none of the disciples seems to notice anything. Are we to suppose that they were so thickheaded that they failed to understand the obvious? And how are we to read the statement that 'after receiving the morsel, Satan entered' into Judas (13:30)? The sentence seems to establish a causal link between the taking of the morsel and the moment of possession by Satan; but it seems unlikely that that was intended. What we can safely assume is that John is torn between two contrary desires. On the one hand, he must tell the story of betrayal in such a way that the disciples are shown to have no inkling about it; otherwise they would, one imagines, be blamed for not having forestalled Judas. But on the other hand, his vision of Jesus implies that he foresaw the betrayal. A short-circuit between Jesus and the disciples is inevitable in such a situation; he who knows and wants to show it without rendering the betrayal impossible, and the disciples who are not supposed to know and yet have the right to a true answer to their questions.

Whatever explanation one wants to give, one startling fact remains: Jesus does not do anything to prevent the betrayal; and one may well wonder why that should be so. The answer of the text seems to be expressed in the words of Jesus immediately after Judas has left: 'Now is the Son of man glorified, and in him God is glorified' (13:31). To glorify (*doxadzo*) is derived from 'glory' (*doxa*). Sometimes, it means 'honour'; as, for example, in 5:44 (to receive honour from man), in 7:18 (to seek one's own glory), or in 9:24 (give praise to God). Sometimes, especially when it is used about God or Jesus it indicates a divine attribute; as, for example in the Prologue, or at Cana where he manifests his glory (see 2:11), or when Lazarus is raised and the disciples see the glory of God (see 11:40). In Hebrew the corresponding term has the connotation of 'weight'. Bearing that in mind, one might render the quotation above as follows: 'Now the Son of man is invested with God's greatness so that God becomes visible in him.' In this perspective Jesus cannot but tolerate Judas' betrayal which will indeed lead to his glorification. Like Caiaphas or Pontius Pilate, Judas plays his preordained role which is to bring about the glorification of Jesus. He is thus seen to fulfil the Scriptures (13:18–19). Viewed from the angle of the participants in the story, Judas' betrayal is a stumbling-block, but viewed from the point of view of the post-paschal believers it is, in fact, a stepping-stone on Jesus' way to glory.

The First Farewell Discourse

Two spatial metaphors describe the relations between the Father and the Son as well as between Jesus and the disciples. The first one is the familiar image opposing the world above and the world below. For the sake of his disciples Jesus interprets the coming events, and he describes them as his going to the Father (14:2 and 14:28). That is a place where the disciples cannot come now (13:36–8), but he is going in advance in order to prepare a place for them (14:2–5). The distance between the world of God and the world of man can also be bridged in another way, by the coming of God to man: 'My Father will love him, and we will come to him and make our home with him' (14:23).

There are, then, two ways to cross the gulf between the two worlds: the one, starting in the world below leads to the Father's house, the other, with its beginning in the world above, brings God to man. At first sight it is not clear whether the way up and the way down are one and the same or whether they are alternative routes. Indeed, the way up requires man to leave the world below, which means to die; in that perspective the union with God lies beyond death. The way down, however, leads to this world in which the presence of God seems mainly an interior one in the souls of the believers; in that perspective the union with God, however invisible except perhaps in the love of the disciples, is already realized in this life, before death. It is easy to see that these two possibilities of interpreting the meeting between God and man have led to the mystical assertion of God's presence here and now and to the hopeful assertion of life eternal. The latter can be understood better when we relate it to the Lazarus episode; the former is to be seen in connection with the second spatial metaphor at work in the text.

This spatial metaphor is based on the preposition 'in'. The Father, says the Gospel in 14:9–11, is in Jesus and does his works, and Jesus is in the Father. Likewise, Jesus is in the believer and the believer is in Jesus (14:20). This 'in' is not a synonym of 'identical'; on the contrary, the distinction between the different persons involved is clearly established, as in the sentence, 'The Father is greater than I' (14:28), or in the assertion that the disciples cannot follow him where he is going. 'In' seems to indicate that the person who is said to be dwelling in another becomes visible in his host. Thus, the Father becomes visible in Jesus' works (14:8ff.), which are indeed the Father's works; the believer who does the works of Jesus will show to all the world that he is a disciple (13:35) if he shares in the love of Jesus (13:34 and 14:12). Doing the works of another might appear as a form of obedience to a command from somebody else; but the 'in' suggests that the will of the guest has as it were been interiorized by the host so that the distinction between one's own desire and the guest's has been obliterated. One is reminded here of the words of Jesus in connection with the spirit and the spring of water welling up to eternal life (see 3:6–8, 4:14 and 7:37–9). It is not surprising, in this context, that mention should be made of the gift of the Advocate who will be sent to the disciples and become the principle of their lives (14:15ff.).

The two spatial metaphors are only partly compatible. They belong to different categories, that of absence for the way up and down, that of presence for the 'in'-sentences. In the first case, the union of God and man is a promise that will be realized through the death of Jesus. In the second case it is already realized. The two statements can be made compatible if the coming of God to man is interpreted as a mystical presence, beyond experience but nonetheless real. The contradiction between the two ways of speaking can also be found on the temporal level. The discourse moves between a promise (the use of the future tense, such as 'you will know' and 'he will be loved') and the confirmation of a present fact (Jesus is already in the Father, and the Father is already in him; likewise, 'the Advocate dwells in you').

Was John aware of this ambiguity and is that the reason why he emphasizes the difference between the two statements in the disciples' knowledge? 'In that day you will know that I am in my Father, and you in me, and I in you' (14:20). That means that the union between the Father and the Son on the one hand, and the union between the Son and the disciples on the other hand, are already a fact, even before the Resurrection, and that it is only the disciples' consciousness that will change. Once again John seems to conflate statements about the situation before the Resurrection and statements about the situation after that event. A historical perspective blends with an eternal one. That is possible because John writes his Gospel when the betrayal and later events of Maundy Thursday might already belong to the past; from one point of view they have happened, from the other one they have not. To formulate this in a slightly different way: Jesus is both the eternal Word and the temporal flesh, beyond time and in time.

The determining factor, as to whether the human being can enter this state of union with God, is his acceptance of Jesus and his willingness to keep Jesus' commandments. The salient word here is 'love', the meaning of which has been demonstrated by Jesus himself when he washed the feet of his disciples. After these explanations, Jesus invites his disciples to 'rise and go hence' (14:31).

The Second Farewell Discourse

As if he were not satisfied with the explanations given by Jesus to interpret the coming events and their importance for human kind, John relates a second farewell speech. As is to be expected, this second discourse repeats a fair number of statements from the first one. It repeats that the Father and the Son are one (15:9–10) and that Jesus is going back to the Father (16:5 and 28). It promises once more that the Spirit will come and testify to Jesus (16:13–15), and it asserts once again the intimate link between the keeping of the commandments and the love of Jesus (15:9ff.). New are the allegory of the vine which needs pruning (15:1–6), the insistence on the gift of one's life (15:12–17), the announcement of conflict and persecutions (15:18—16:4), further details about the function of the Holy Spirit (16:5–15), and the explicit warning about

71

Jesus' own Passion and its repercussions on the lives of the disciples (16:16–33).

The theme is broached in the allegory of the vine. That motif goes back to the Old Testament; there the people of Israel are compared to a vineyard planted and tended by God. In Jesus' version of that old image he is the vine; with this starting-point the people are necessarily compared to the branches which will bear fruit only when they are connected with the stem. Jesus, the vine, and the people, the branches, form the new vineyard, the new Israel. But that idea is not developed; all the stress is laid on the necessary conjunction between vine and branches and on the bearing of fruit. Obviously, this is a variation on the ideas expressed in the 'in'-metaphor of the first discourse.

The way this is done is characteristic of John's theological style. It proceeds slowly, repeating a statement again and again, sometimes with small changes that prepare for the introduction of a new key-word. An example will show this clearly. In the two basic statements of the allegory Jesus is called the vine, the Father the vine-dresser, and the disciples the branches (15:1 and 5). The allegory is then worked out in detail. The injunction, 'Abide in me as I in you' (15:4), is transformed into 'He who abides in me and I in him' (15:5); it is then modified into a conditional statement, 'If a man does not abide in me' (15:6), repeated in the affirmative, 'If you abide in me, and my words abide in you' (15:7). In this last version 'my words' can be considered as a metonymy for the speaker (in the usage of the word which combines metonymy in the strict sense and synecdoche).

That prepares the way for another metonymy: 'abide in my love' (15:9), introducing the new keyword 'love' and opening up the way for a new development centring on that keyword. 'If you keep my commandments you will abide in my love' (15:10) leads to the definition of the commandment: 'This is my commandment that you love one another' (15:12). That commandment is clarified by an example which is at the same time a prophecy involving Jesus himself: 'Greater love has no man than this that a man lay down his life for his *friends*. You are my *friends* if you do what I command you.

No longer do I call you *servants*, for the *servant* ... I have
called you *friends*' (15:13–15) (italics mine); and the passage
ends with the repetition of the basic commandment: 'This I
command you, to love one another' (15:17). This is then
followed by a passage in which 'hate', the antonym of 'love',
becomes the key-word to explain the attitude of the Jews and
their rejection of Jesus (see 15:18–25).

This redundant, associative style is, of course, very slow
and meditative. The message it brings can be briefly summarized. There is, as the 'in'-passages of the first discourse have
already indicated, a deep unity between the Father and the
Son on the one hand, and between the Son and the believers
on the other hand. The principle of unity is 'love'. The meaning of love can be seen in the example of the man giving his
life for his friends, also in the keeping of the commandments;
and among these commandments is the order 'to witness to
Jesus' (see 15:27 and, though less sure, 15:16). To abide in
Jesus' love it is, then, not sufficient to lead a virtuous life,
one must also bear witness to him who is the living example
of love: 'Love one another as I have loved you' (15:12).

If Jesus has suffered for being what he is, the disciples,
who follow in his footsteps, can expect the same treatment,
motivated by the same hatred (see 15:18–25). But Jesus consoles his disciples with the certainty of victory over the
powers of darkness (see 14:30, 16:20ff. and 16:33). On the one
hand he will send them the Counsellor (16:7), on the other
hand he promises to come back himself (16:20ff.). The contradiction requires elucidation. 'When the Spirit comes' (16:8)
he will clearly show, first, that the world has committed a sin
by refusing Jesus, secondly, that Jesus is the prototype of
righteousness because he goes to the Father, and, thirdly, that
the 'ruler of this world is judged' (16:9–10). In other words,
it will be clear whose side God is on. 'When he comes'
(16:13), he will guide the disciples into all truth and declare
to them 'the things that are to come' (16:13; see also 14:26).

These promises seem to bear on the life of the disciples
after Jesus has left them. But what can then be the meaning
of the other statements asserting that he will leave them,
but after a short while come back for ever? Many possible

readings present themselves: he might be talking about the short period between his death and the first appearances after Easter; or he might be talking about what tradition has called the Second Coming at the end of time; or he might be referring to the mystical coming of the Father and the Son which he had promised (see 14:23–4); or about the three possible interpretations at the same time. The problem is made even more complex by the fact that the Spirit is sometimes described as already present and yet still to come (see 14:17: 'for he dwells with you, and will be in you').

Jesus' Prayer

The chapter which follows is generally known under the name 'the priestly prayer'. Indeed, Jesus no longer addresses his disciples, but the Father himself. Apart from verses 2 and 3, in which he speaks about himself in the third person, throughout the text he is an 'I' facing his Father as a 'You'. That determines the status of this discourse; it is not merely recording what happens, it creates what it expresses; in one word, it is performative speech in which Jesus constitutes himself as the Son. Knowing that Jesus is the Son and that he has received authority over all creation so that he can give eternal life, the evangelist daringly describes the most intimate thoughts of Jesus.

'The hour has come' (17:1). The Gospel mentions a number of 'hours', as, for example, the 'tenth hour' at the disciples' first meeting with Jesus; but equally often it stresses the fact that 'his hour has not yet come' and that it is too early for his glory to be made manifest (at Cana). Now, that decisive hour has come and Father and Son will be glorified. One should remember that that has already happened – for example, at Cana and with Lazarus. And yet this is a special hour at which the glorification will be absolute. In verse 5 Jesus asks to be glorified in the Father's presence with the glory he had 'before the world was made'. Looking back beyond creation, the reader envisages the beginning before the beginning, the Being of God himself which is revealed to the world. This hour is, therefore, more than the decisive hour announcing the beginning of, say, a campaign; it is the hour when the Eternal enters the world of time and God's own being is made visible in mortal man. 'The Word become flesh', which began with the birth of Jesus, is here brought to its ultimate completion, because that which was still hidden at that moment is here made manifest; this is the hour of hours.

It is a turning-point. Knowing that he will no longer remain in the world, Jesus looks back on the work he has accomplished and forward to the future of his disciples. But that is not the most striking feature of this text. Its most impressive characteristic is its incantatory repetition of some formulae. The formula that occurs most frequently is the designation of his disciples as the men 'whom thou gavest me out of this world' which is repeated no less than twelve times. Besides, there are relative clauses 'whom/which thou gavest me' with another antecedent such as 'the work, the glory, the words'. Another frequent phrase 'that thou has sent me' occurs in verses 3, 8, 21 and 23. Moreover, there is the insistent use of parallelism, often introduced by 'as'. A few examples will do: 'They are not of the world, even as I am not of the world' (v.16); 'As thou didst send me into the world, so I have sent them into the world' (v.18) and 'I consecrate myself that they may also be consecrated in truth' (v.19).

This typical style influences the communication. It confuses the reader, because the repetitions make it difficult for him to follow the thread of the argument; he never knows whether the information is new or redundant. But on the other hand that same repetition imparts the suggestion that the terms 'I, you, they' belong together and cannot be separated. Their relation is the gist of what is being communicated. A glance at the keywords confirms this. Take 'to glorify': it is an action of the Father (17:1 and 5), but it is also an action of the Son (17:1 and 4), and the faithful are its beneficiaries. 'To send' is an activity of Father and Son, and both the Son and the believers are sent (see 17:3, 18, 21). The same pattern is seen if one looks at terms like 'keep' or 'love'; 'to keep' is an activity of the Father and of the Son and it benefits the disciples (17:11–12) whom the Father and the Son love

75

equally. There is, then, as the text suggests, an endless divine activity, both between Father and Son, and between the Son and his own. But this inherence of the Son in the Father and of the disciples in Jesus also manifests itself at the level of being. 'They are not of the world, even as I am not of the world,' Jesus says in verse 14 and again in verse 16; he wants them to be with the Father as he is himself (17:24); and they will be one, even as Jesus and the Father are one (17:11). The culminating statement is not the last sentence of the speech, but the awe-inspiring 'As thou, Father, art in me, and I in thee, that they also may be in us' (17:21).

At the source of this unity between the Father and the Son and the disciples lies the divine initiative of the Father who sends the Son. In a sense, this decision has already been carried out. Jesus has glorified God (17:4), he has manifested the Name (17:6), communicated the message (17:8); the disciples have accepted this message and therefore they do not belong to this world. But they still live in a world which does not accept Jesus; they are called upon to witness to him, and in that activity they will, like Jesus, have to confront the cross.

FRIDAY: PASSION AND DEATH (18:1—19:42)

The story of the Passion can be divided into four sections: the arrest in the garden, the mock trial, the crucifixion and the burial.

The Arrest in the Garden

Although Jesus is the detainee, he keeps the initiative. He is confronted with a posse composed of soldiers and temple officers, which suggests an alliance of the political and religious authorities, and they are led by the traitor. Resistance would be heroic, but it is bound to be unsuccessful; Peter's ill-judged attempt at resistance is futile. And yet Jesus, 'knowing all that would befall him, came forward' (18:4) and revealed his identity. The words he uses have resounded each time he solemnly manifested himself; here too he declares, 'I am', and the text repeats the formula three times, in verses 5, 6 and 8. Moreover, he requests – and gets – a safe-conduct for his disciples (18:8) and he quietens Peter down; his words are so impressive that the soldiers 'drew back and fell to the ground' (18:6). If he wished, the text suggests, he could avoid being arrested; and one remembers the many times when they tried to arrest or stone him and nobody laid hands on him. If he is arrested, the story implies, it is because he permits it; and he permits it, because that is the cup which the Father has given him (see 18:11). It is as if the Father had decided that Jesus was to suffer and as if the soldiers were merely instruments bringing about the passion. That is difficult to accept. But the idea becomes somewhat more palatable if one interprets it against the background of earlier sayings of Jesus in the farewell discourses. Jesus has been sent to fulfil a mission and he has accepted to accomplish it whatever the cost; if he wills what the Father wills, he also wills this Passion which is linked with the mission, not in principle but in fact. His consent thus reveals the gratuitous boundless love of the Father and the Son who want to share life with human kind.

The Mock Trial

Jesus is taken prisoner and is brought first before the Jewish authorities and afterwards before the Roman magistrate. The interrogation does not yield any results. Jesus repeats what he has been saying all along. His own question on what he did wrong (see 18:23) does not get an answer either, which shows that nothing can be brought against him. In the mean time the personal drama of Peter unfolds in the wings, under-scoring Jesus' solitude and, by contrast, his greatness. In scenes such as this (18:15–18, 25–7), where men interact, John displays a realism which would grace a contemporary short story. But as soon as he introduces Jesus he abandons all attempts at realism (in our sense of the word) and proceeds to lay bare a hidden reality. The interrogation by Pontius Pilate offers a good example of this change in style. It begins with a contest between Pilate and the Jews about questions of jurisdiction; and it is rendered in straightforward language. As soon, however, as Jesus enters the scene the tone changes. Now, words are used with plural meanings, and sayings move on at least two levels at the same time. Take the word 'king': it is used literally by Pontius Pilate, but it becomes a metaphor in the mouth of Jesus who is indeed a king but not in the way of this world (18:36), and it is used ironically by the soldiers who taunt him. When the Jews deny him, and cry out, 'We have no king but Caesar,' they speak the truth unwittingly, for in rejecting him they prove that they have opted for the world; and when Pilate calls Jesus 'the King of the Jews', what is meant as an insult becomes a deep truth, for this ill-treated suffering man is the King.

This description of the trial incriminates the Jews and tends to exculpate Pilate. He appears as an outsider who gets reluctantly implicated in what seems to him a typically Jewish quarrel over trifles, the implications of which escape him. He performs his task correctly, until he gives in to the Jews' blackmail even though he is convinced of Jesus' innocence; and that shows that he belongs to this world, too.

The Crucifixion

In total conformity with Jesus' active role in the Passion, 'He bears his own cross' (19:17), without assistance from anybody. On the cross he keeps the initiative when he entrusts his mother and the beloved disciple to one another (see 19:24–7); and when he dies 'he bowed his head and gave up his spirit' (19:30). This expression can be read in two ways: either it means 'he expired', or it means 'in dying he gave the Spirit' whom he had promised. This interpretation may seem farfetched, but there are strong arguments to support it. The original Greek reads 'pneuma', which means both 'breath and spirit'; and, moreover, it is borne out by the general drift of the Gospel for which the death of Jesus and the mission of the Spirit are simultaneous events. This moment of utter defeat becomes then, paradoxically, the moment of complete glorification.

The evangelist has taken great pains to illustrate this truth.

Not only does he avoid all mention of the nerve-racking physical and moral suffering, but he uses whatever detail he can to point to the glorification.

There is, first, Pontius Pilate's ironic inscription which turns out to be true; there is, furthermore, the detail of the seamless tunic which is not torn up (19:23–4), and the fact that, in contrast with the usual practice, Jesus' legs remain unbroken (19:31–3); and, finally, 'the flow of blood and water' (19:34) from his pierced side. In the light of Jesus' promise of the living water or of his sayings about his blood, this apparent detail has a symbolic meaning. Not only did blood and water play a major role in Jesus' teaching, they are also important symbols in the life of the Church. The water is, once and for all, the symbol used in baptism to incorporate the individual in the Church and to give the newly baptized person a part in God's life; and the blood calls to mind the Eucharist which is the centre of the life of the Church. Therefore, the flow of water and blood from the pierced side of Jesus has always been interpreted as the foundation of the Church. Just as with the sending of the holy Spirit, the foundation of the Church coincides with the moment of Jesus' death. The hour of his death is the hour of birth of the Church.

In this context one also understands Jesus' words to his mother and the beloved disciple. In his farewell discourses he had stressed the unity between him and his disciples. Here that unity is given a concrete shape. Mary becomes for the disciple what she had been for Jesus; and the disciple becomes what Jesus was for her. So great is the unity that the disciple, in a sense, replaces Jesus and becomes his deputy. That, too, is the Church, a living community in which each member is in Jesus and Jesus in him.

The many quotations from the Scriptures belong here. If this is the climax of God's revelation, it must be in conformity with God's action and therefore also with Scripture which records that action. These quotations show the continuity in God's action, but they also demand a new interpretation. Old Testament fragments yield their full significance only when they are related to Jesus.

The Burial

Jesus might have been buried in another way, but, as the glorification motive requires, he was buried in 'a new tomb where no one had ever been laid' (19:41). And he is buried with all the honours the Jewish customs provide. It is also fitting that Nicodemus who had failed to recognize Jesus when he was alive should be the one who recognizes him in his death (see 19:39) and brings the mixture of myrrh and aloes to enbalm the body.

THE EIGHTH DAY

APPEARANCES OF THE RISEN LORD (Chapter 20)

THE SABBATH is over, the new week has begun. It is new in more than the conventional sense. For the appearances of the Risen Christ, together with the gift of the Spirit and the mission of the disciples, inaugurate a new era in our history. Jesus' words about the new temple, the new human being and the new life are now confirmed.

There are, as one would expect, three appearances recorded in Saint John's Gospel: one to Mary Magdalene early in the morning when it is still dark (20:1); one to the assembled apostles (Thomas being absent) in the evening of that same day (20:19), and one a week later to the apostles when Thomas is with them (20:26). Whether the time-indications have a symbolical or a merely chronological function cannot be ascertained. It is, however, generally admitted that the chronologies of the four gospels diverge so much that an exact chronology of the appearances cannot be reconstructed. The feeling predominates that the evangelists were guided by theological motives rather than by a wish for historical precision. One might therefore surmise that the time indications have a symbolic function, but there are, as far as I can see, not enough indications in the text to allow for more than guesses.

To Mary Magdalene

The whole story begins with the discovery of an absence; the tomb is empty. That does not necessarily imply that Jesus has risen. It might indicate that he has disappeared in death and that nothing of him remains. Mary Magdalene is the first to discover the emptiness of the tomb, but she recognizes the authority of the apostles and first goes to tell them. There is some uncertainty as to who brings the news; the story says explicitly that it is Mary Magdalene, but in her message to the apostles she speaks of 'we' which would indicate that she was not all by herself. This may be traced back to the Gospel's sources, but one has to explain why John has reduced the multiplicity to one. However that may be, Mary has a negative message to bring: 'The Lord is not where we thought he was.'

Later she will become the bearer of the good news that she has seen the Lord (20:18). She is the crown witness. Why she has been given such an important part to play, can only be guessed. But that she has this part, is beyond all doubt. Together with Mary, with the Samaritan woman and with Martha and Mary she represents women in the history of Jesus and his followers. She is the first to recognize him after his death, just as the Samaritan woman was the first of her nation to believe in him; and because of her love for Jesus Mary Magdalene is often confused with Lazarus' sister who anointed Jesus' feet.

The reaction of the apostles is significant. Peter is slower than the other disciple, both in getting to the tomb and in drawing conclusions. Of the other it is said that he 'went into the tomb, and he saw and believed' (20:8); but there is no mention of Peter's faith. Yet he is given his due, and his special position among the apostles is recognized: he is the first to enter the tomb and to notice the orderly way in which the linen cloths and the napkin have been rolled up. It is as if, in contrast with Lazarus, Jesus had not been bound by the cerements but had disposed of them and left the tomb quietly. That Peter cannot draw the same conclusion as the other disciple may be due to the fact that 'they did not know the Scripture' (20:9). But the pronoun in the plural seems to put them both into the same category. Be that as it may, the text certainly, if implicitly, suggests that the resurrection can only be thought of within the framework of the Scriptures. They are not sufficient to engender faith, but they are a necessary condition for faith. The one who accepts the Scriptures believes indeed in a God of life who will never abandon his servant Son. But, as so often in this Gospel, the words of Scripture require interpretation; and one might argue that the disciple whom Jesus loved, is – in this account – more attuned to the spirit of the text and therefore quicker in perceiving the message.

Mary is still lost, weeping. The two angels she sees in the tomb do not have the important function of announcing the resurrection which they have in the Synoptics. They content themselves with the sympathetic question, 'Why are you weeping?' (20:13), which may be understood as suggesting that there is no cause for tears. That is borne out by the appearance of Christ himself. As in most stories about the appearances, the encounter is characterized by an initial non-recognition, as if he had become so different as to prevent recognition, or as if the disciples so little expected the resurrection that it was beyond their imagining. It is the word of Christ, his forgiving, life-giving word as we have come to know it in the diverse episodes in this Gospel, that brings about recognition. The disciple's insight, expressed in the word 'Rabboni', dawns as the light of Christ manifests itself: he is the first to speak; she responds. It is, however, typical that she uses the word 'Teacher' to address him, as if she thought that the relationship between them was still the same as it had been during his lifetime.

The words of Jesus, 'Do not hold me,' indicate that their relationship has entered a new stage. He is no longer among them, but, to use the familiar topographical metaphor, he is 'ascending to my Father and your Father' (20:17). The phrase harks back to the farewell discourses with their insistence on the unity between the Father and the Son and the disciples. Here it is especially the unity between Father and Son that is stressed.

So the story of Mary Magdalene reveals a first truth about Jesus: he is with the Father. How, then, can he also be with the disciples who are still in this world? The answer to that question is given in the appearance of Jesus to the disciples.

To the Disciples

That story is very short indeed; and it is, like the previous one, surprisingly sober and matter of fact. The risen Lord sends his disciples: 'As the Father sent me, even so I send you' (20:21). One ought to remember here that in this Gospel the notion of sending is a special one, in that the one who is sending remains active in the one that is being sent. When the Father sends Jesus, the Father abides in him so that to see Jesus is to see the Father. Similarly, Christ is united with his disciples so that they do what he does and he works through them. That was the gist of the discourses on Maundy Thursday, 'you in me and I in them'. That is why they are baptized in the Holy Spirit and promised the power of forgiving sins. They can, in the name of Christ (that is, in his place), leave the old world behind and enter the new life, reborn. This second appearance thus brings an additional message: where the appearance to Mary Magdalene shows that Jesus is with the Father, this appearance stresses the fact that he remains with them, in a new way certainly but nonetheless really and effectively present. The meaning of this presence has never been better explained than in the following lines by the English poet, Gerard Manley Hopkins:

> For Christ plays in ten thousand places,
> Lovely in limbs, and lovely in eyes not his
> To the Father through the features of men's faces.*

To Thomas and the Disciples

In order to answer Thomas' doubts, the Lord appears once more, a week after his first appearance. Thomas is fascinated by the wounds. He wants, as it were, to make sure that the One his fellow-disciples have seen is really the One who has suffered and died on a cross. He expects nothing from a word that has not become flesh and has not shared the human predicament. But when he realizes that this is indeed and recognizably Jesus, with the scars of his suffering visible

* From 'As Kingfishers Catch Fire'.

and tangible in his glorified body, he expresses his faith in the words in which this Gospel culminates: 'My Lord and my God!' (20:28). These words, which have become a model for all the later generations of Christians, embody the fullness of faith in Christ. One might say that this third appearance is mentioned less for what it reveals about the risen Christ than for what it tells about the human response to him. But that would be an exaggerated claim. For this passage reminds us of what we always want to forget: Jesus' suffering was no accident but is part and parcel of his mission, so much so that its tell-tale scars have been inscribed on his body. The risen Christ who is for ever with the Father and, in the Spirit, with his disciples is the one who has suffered; Christ is for ever the 'Christus passus'. That is why the cross is the sign of his glorification.

These three appearances might have an apologetic function, and it is true that they are often read in that light. But their thrust goes in another direction; they all show where the Christ is now. One remembers the initial question of the apostles at the very beginning of the Gospel: 'Rabbi, where are you staying?' (1:39) They have followed him and learned the answer to that question; and the reader of the Gospel has gone along with them. It was a slow process of enlightenment, a patient reading of signs that did not immediately yield their message, a baffling experience which went against much that had been taken for granted. In sign after sign, seven in all, new aspects of his being were brought to the fore and interpreted.

The sign of the cross is the last of all, the final one. It tells us how the suffering servant Jesus is now with God and yet at the same time present in his disciples through the Spirit he sends; their actions are his actions, his suffering is also theirs. This truth is not an empirical truth; to accept it is first and foremost an act of faith. But then 'blessed are those who have not seen and yet believe' (20:29). And yet the presence of Christ in this world can sometimes be experienced. Was it because that aspect of Christian life had not been clearly enough expounded, that the Evangelist (or another writer) felt the need to add one more passage? Was this Gospel clearly meant to end with the statement: 'These are written that you may believe that Jesus is the Christ, the Son of God, and that believing you may have life in his name' (20:31)? We shall never know the answers to these questions. But that the final chapter 21 adds a new element to the faith in Christ is beyond doubt.

EPILOGUE

APPEARANCE AT THE LAKESIDE AND THE MISSION OF THE APOSTLES (ch.21)

THE WRITER of the text calls this the third appearance to the disciples; that he ignores the appearance to Mary Magdalene may be an oversight, but it is more likely that he wanted to play down the woman's role. After all only the apostles had the authority! His account of the appearance is introduced by the bald statement 'and he revealed himself in this way' (21:1), by the names of those involved and the mention that the apostles had gone back to their former occupation, fishing. The description itself contains a number of contradictions which makes it difficult to read the story realistically. Leaving aside the fact that the disciples do not recognize Jesus, which is a common theme to all the resurrection stories, there remain a few anomalies in the description. It seems strange that Peter should put on his clothes before springing into the sea, or that he is able single-handed to haul ashore the net which had previously been too heavy for the disciples to haul in. Equally surprising is the fact that Jesus already has fish ready for them, or the disciples' unwillingness to ask their guest 'Who are you?' and the reason for that unwillingness, 'They knew it was the Lord' (21:12).

These inconsistencies may be due to a certain clumsiness which makes itself felt, especially towards the end of the chapter, but they may also invite to a more figurative reading. One will remember the idea put forward in the Synoptics that fishing is a symbol for the apostolic activity; when Jesus calls his apostles he tells them that he will make them fishers of men. In the present story they haul in a large quantity of fish, which seems to symbolize the apostolic activity. In its success Christ's presence can be experienced.

Two arguments militate in favour of this interpretation. The idyllic image of the meal at the lakeside in the early morning with Christ as the host for his bemused apostles is as it were an anticipation of the new world which the apostolic activity labours to bring about. But, and this is more important, the rest of the chapter is devoted to ecclesiastic matters. There is the question of Peter's betrayal and there is the question of his relation to that mysterious one 'whom Jesus loved'. Peter is not allowed to forget his behaviour on Maundy Thursday, but he is nevertheless charged with the apostolic mission of feeding the sheep in the name of the Good Shepherd himself after he has expressed his love of Jesus. His martyrdom contrasts with the longevity of the other disciple, but this Gospel, which probably originated in a Johannine church, is at pains to show that that other disciple is in no way Peter's inferior, even if he had to go without the crown of martyrdom.

After this reminder of the fraternal quarrels in the early Church, the Gospel ends on a naive admission of defeat. What the Gospel has tried to describe is too great for words. Jesus cannot be locked up in books; he is always beyond them, that is, always beyond what men might think or write about him. He is greater than our thoughts and than our hearts. And that may well be the ultimate cause of the disciples' unwillingness to ask, 'Who are you?' They knew it was the Lord.

LOOKING BACK

T EXTS ARE INEXHAUSTIBLE. Unchanging though they are in the materiality of the printed signs, they keep changing in their meaning. Great religious and secular texts always seem to contain more meanings than their interpreters had imagined; and their interpretations are never final or definitive. They are indeed approached with new questions, related to new issues, framed by a new context and projected against a new horizon of understanding; and that changes them. Moreover, what T.S. Eliot said about the work of art which takes its place among already existing works and thereby changes their relative position, is also valid for texts. And that explains why commentaries continue to be written, even if their writers are aware of their necessarily provisional character.

This book offers a commentary which considers the Gospel as a text, and studies it with the methods and concepts that have been introduced into literary studies in the last fifty years. More specifically it asks how meaning comes into being, and which linguistic devices dominate the text and determine its sense. On the basis of the analysis in the previous chapters, it is possible to distinguish three styles in John's Gospel. There is, to begin with, the straightforward factual narrative characterized by a high degree of verisimilitude; examples of this realistic style are the account of the discussion between the man born blind and the Jews in chapter 9, and that of the altercation between Peter and the personnel of the high priest in chapter 18. But another style predominates in the commentaries and in most narratives involving Jesus. Whenever the text reports his words or his actions, it abandons the realistic mode and uses some literary devices, forcing the reader to look for a more than literal meaning; here we find John's own narrative style. That same technique, together with the lyrical use of repetition and variation of words and phrases, can be found in the doctrinal comments; and that is John's theological style. In these two styles the major linguistic operation is the displacement of meaning; and that is brought about by the use of metaphor on the semantic level and the use of paradox, irony and quotation on the logical level.

Metaphors blend terms which belong to mutually exclusive categories; therefore some theorists define the metaphor as a category mistake. For example, in the metaphor, 'I am the vine', the human person is described in terms belonging to the realm of plants. The referent (that is, the object in the non-linguistic reality) is no vine, and yet it can be called just that; it is and it is not a vine. It is for the reader to decide in which sense the term 'vine' is valid in the given statement and in which sense it is not. Metaphor is the opposite of a definition; it does not determine what the referent is, but it sets one thinking in a certain direction.

How much that is the case here can be inferred from the attempt to define the sense of the vehicle 'vine' in its metaphorical usage. It will soon appear that there are no satisfactory synonyms for it, but that a series of paraphrases is called for. When one tries to combine two metaphors which have the same tenor (or referent), the situation becomes even more complicated. Thus Jesus says of himself that he is the vine, but also that he is the shepherd. The relation of the sheep to the shepherd differs from the relation between vine and branches; and each image has its own logic. The 'shepherd' metaphor introduces the ideas of 'following', of 'mutual knowledge', of 'independence', whereas the 'vine' metaphor calls up associations of 'pruning', 'growing', 'bearing fruit'. To pursue the logic of one vehicle to the end leads into unsurmountable difficulties. Taking the example of the vine, one might think that the yearly shedding of leaves is part of the meaning of the referent. But to go hunting for all the possible applications of the vehicle leads one into allegory; and that would, at least in the present case, be a dead end.

There are, indeed, too many conflicting metaphors to indicate Jesus. He is, in succession, 'light, water, bread, temple, shepherd, the door of the pen, the bridegroom, the son'. Each of these terms can be used as a predicate in connection with Christ, and each of them adds new elements to our understanding of him. What is relevant and what is not, must be carefully weighed, so as to avoid conflicts, and yet, even conflicting statements have their importance, as they show that Jesus is not to be pinned down to a single formula. Metaphors are there to make one think; they use elements from the familiar world, which are well known to the audience, and use them as lamps on the way to the unknown, reaching for the light. The vehicles of the metaphorical meaning are concepts that can be used to predicate something of the tenor. When only the concept is used, there is metaphor; when the referent is meant we have a symbol. Thus, the concept 'water' is a metaphor for Christ, but the element (in nature) becomes a symbol for everything Christ can offer man and which is more than even the concept 'water' can suggest. Whether a term is used in a metaphorical sense or as the name of a symbol, one must in either case go beyond a literal understanding. 'It is the spirit that gives life, the letter is of no avail.'

A second style-figure which transcends the literal meaning is the *paradox*. Here something is said or done which goes against the grain of common opinion. Its major literary device is the oxymoron: the conjunction of two mutually exclusive concepts, preferably of a noun with an adjective that denies an essential trait of the noun it is associated with; thus, for example, 'the living dead' or 'the dark light'. This is a frequent device in the spiritual writings of many religious traditions, especially in mystic ones. It does not occur as such in John. What we do find is the simultaneous affirmation of two irreconcilable statements. That the crucifixion, which is a punishment reserved for criminals, is the sign of Jesus' glorification is such a paradox; that the tree of death is the tree of life is another. Those are paradoxical combinations of meaning, and they are unlikely. Equally unlikely, but even more frequent is the combination of irreconcilable facts: he is glorified and he must still be glorified; he is above the manoeuvres of the Jews and yet he is taken prisoner; he will send the holy Spirit and the Spirit is already there. These and similar paradoxes are merely manifestations of that one great paradox which the whole Gospel is meant to elucidate: 'the Word become flesh'. Here two antonymous terms are fused in a superior unity. Perhaps the best formulation of that paradox is T.S. Eliot's verse in *Four Quartets*:

> Here the impossible union
> Of spheres of existence is actual,
> Here the past and the future
> Are conquered and reconciled.

This sense of paradox which pervade the Gospel forces the reader to abandon the level of rational understanding and to reach out for a meaning and a reality which transcend his thoughts. It functions, on its level, in the same way and with the same effect as the metaphor does on its level.

Irony works in a similar fashion. It changes the meaning of what is said or written into its contrary. When one tries to reformulate the ironic statement into a straightforward one, one discovers that more than one paraphrase is needed to do justice to the text. Take for instance the cry of the Jews: 'We have no king but Caesar.' The cry contradicts what they profess to believe – namely, that God is their sole God. It serves as a form of pressure to persuade Pontius Pilate to do what they want him to do, and as such it is merely a tactical lie. But at the same time it describes their existential situation in that their rejection of Jesus proves that they belong to this world, the world of Caesar. They lie, yet they speak the truth. But the irony is not visible in the text; it is not announced by any diacritical sign. If it is discovered, it is thanks to the perceptiveness of the reader. Once again the letter of the text will not do; it must be read in the right spirit.

The play with *quotations* is another frequent device. A quotation is an alien element in the text; it belongs elsewhere,

92

but yet it is used to underscore or to illustrate the message with all the weight of its authority. It is characteristic of John's use of quotations that they are not understood when they are brought forward. Their real meaning is discovered after Jesus' passion and resurrection. They are, then, used in a new context, and what they were believed to say gives way to a new understanding. The literal meaning is replaced by a spiritual one.

The first three figures of speech considered above all create meaning by a linguistic operation which was well known in classical rhetoric. This operation, which is one of the four possible operations, simultaneously suppresses some linguistic traits and introduces new ones; it is the operation of *suppressio/adjunctio*. Thus in the statement, 'I am the vine', some semantic traits (/vegetal/, /gnarled/, /bound to one place/, etc.) are deleted while other ones (/human/, /freedom of decision/, /choice of a life-style/) are imported. For a fuller discussion of these linguistic operations, the reader will find a rich source of information in *Rhétorique générale*.* For our purpose here it suffices to observe that the text is clearly inspired by a specific stylistic option. That John so frequently uses the same mental operation is symptomatic of his way of thinking. For him the reality of Jesus is more complex and more surprising than one would think at first sight. There is more here than meets the eye. What one sees is both a screen and a window, transparent and yet a veil, concealing and revealing at the same time.

In the Gospel John projects an image of himself as the one who knows. He reveals what is hidden; and therefore tradition has always considered him as the author of the book of Revelation as well. Moreover, he is a member of a group which shares his opinions, and which has learnt to see the reality beyond the reality. In stark contrast with Pontius Pilate's sceptical question, 'What is truth?', John and his community believe that they have 'the spirit and the truth'. They have received the Spirit who has made them see the meaning of the personality and life of Jesus. That being the case, it no

* Compiled at Liège University and published by Larousse, 1970.

longer matters who bears witness to Christ; whether Jesus speaks or the evangelist or the Christian community, it is always the same Spirit who is at work. The Gospel can therefore erase the difference between the various witnesses, and attribute to one speaker what it might equally well have attributed to another one.

It goes without saying that such a view, which distinguishes the one who sees from the one who does not, runs the risk of gnosticism. And indeed gnostic tendencies have always referred to this Gospel to defend their position. But then, this is but one of the four Gospels. John, who has used the other three Gospels and who, as our reading has shown, often presupposes them, speaks with such an assurance that one might be tempted to believe that he has a deeper apprehension and a more valid understanding of the mystery of Jesus than the other evangelists; what is difficult often seems deep and therefore truer than what is lucid. But one ought to remember that this Gospel, as much as the other three, is an interpretation; and as such, it is not to be given precedence over them, however deep and sublime it is. There are four Gospels; and therefore, the reader of John's Gospel must always look at the other Gospels as well in order to discover, through the prism of their variety, the Lord whom they have interpreted for the ages.

The differences between them are great. If one were to describe their formal difference in an image, the Synoptics could be likened to a film, a straightforward narrative in a simple chronological order and giving great attention to the events and their succession. John, however, makes one think of a lecture with slides: a few well chosen slides, depicting events, are projected in a somewhat haphazard order and accompanied by commentaries of varying length in the form of dialogues or of monologues.

But it is especially on the thematic level that the differences are significant. The Synoptics, one might argue, show us a human Jesus, who is tempted, who suffers and who dies in agony. The One whom John depicts is more the Christ of faith. Hieratically sublime, he is not tempted in the desert, he suffers no agony in the Garden of Gethsemane or on the cross, and his bones are not broken; he shows few emotions, except perhaps his will to serve the Father; his way of speaking is solemn, even when he refers to daily objects or daily situations. Instead of drawing another picture of the man Jesus, John, like his symbol the eagle, pierces the sky and sees the heavens open; he shows the origin of Christ in God and his being one with the Father. Whether the Prologue is written by John or by a later author as many exegetes think, it certainly sets the tone for the rest of the Gospel; it also indicates the spirit in which the Gospel must be read. The Gospel will try to show how the Word has taken on a human figure and through the flesh manifests himself. In John's view the divine character of Jesus shines through the curtain of flesh, already in this world. As soon as he enters the scene he invites the people to come and see; his actions are so many signs of what lies beyond the flesh, and his words reveal him. One might be tempted to look for a progression in this self-revelation, but what one finds is that the whole reality is already there right from the start.

In his interpretation of Jesus' life John shows us, simultaneously, Jesus in time and Jesus in God's eternity; Jesus speaks of the past from which he comes, of the future he is about to enter, and yet, at the same time, he is at one with God in an eternal present; he is already glorified at Cana and yet awaits further glorification. This paradoxical message tends to erase the distinction between the pre-paschal Jesus and the post-paschal Christ; and it seems to erase the distinction between the time before and after the Incarnation. John does not attach much importance to chronology. As a result the historic event – as, for example, the Samaritan woman's meeting with Jesus – acquires a typological dimension; it manifests the structure of the meeting with Christ, at any place, any time. Therefore the believer can identify with the characters in the Gospel. The Incarnation which took place two thousand years ago, is also a continuing process; and so is the Resurrection. It happens every day, as Christ sends his spirit. They who listen to the Spirit, hear the Word that spoke there and then and which has not stopped speaking. For the person who listens to this Word, the future holds the promise of eternal life.

It is to this faith that the fourth Gospel bears witness. Its message has imprinted itself on the page in the unchanging materiality of the letter, but it also transcends the letter's literal meaning and constitutes the realm of the Spirit where the winds of inspiration blow, bringing life.

APPENDIX

1: THE FORMAL CHARACTERISTICS OF THE TEXT

FORMAL CHARACTERISTICS, such as the division of a text into chapters, the narrative perspective, the repetition of words, phrases and syntactical patterns, the choice of figures of speech and style, all guide us in our approach to the text and influence the ensuing interpretation. Some of these characteristics can be considered as they occur in the text, but some of them have a bearing on the text as a whole. That is the case for the Gospel's overall structure and for the narrative point of view, which will be considered here.

The Structure of the Story and the Indications of Time

The now familiar division into chapters and verses was introduced at a fairly late date. In the fourth century Eusebius of Caesarea still found it necessary to establish the so-called *Canon Tables*, references for comparison among numbered sections of the Gospels. Several other, often very complicated, systems were used until the thirteenth century when Stephanus Langton, who was to become Archbishop of Canterbury, devised the present division into chapters; it was first used in a Paris Bible of 1226. The numbering of the verses, as we know it today, came into being in the sixteenth century. Obviously, the present division is but one of the many ways to structure the text; and other ways can be tried. This is what most commentaries do, whether they base themselves on thematic units, or on formal indications of time, on changes of place, on changes in the protagonist's activity, or on a combination of these elements.

After John's remarkably detailed chronology in the first week, one expects that a chronological concern will order the text. But that proves to be a mistake. The text refers a couple of times to Jewish feast-days, and further limits itself to the vaguest of time-indicators. The phrase *meta tauta* or *meta touto* (meaning 'after that') occurs a number of times, and each time it can be linked with a change in Jesus' activity and a change in locale. Thus, the first 'after that' (2:12) precedes a long section including his first journey to Jerusalem where he will cleanse the temple and speak to Nicodemus. The second 'after that' (3:22) introduces his travels through Judea and Samaria and his return to Galilee where he does his second sign, healing the official's son. The third 'after that' (5:1) sees his second journey to Jerusalem and the third sign, the healing of the lame man. The fourth 'after that' (6:1) brings Jesus back to Galilee, where the fourth sign, the multiplication of the loaves, is given. The fifth 'after that' (7:1) announces his last journey to Jerusalem and the fifth sign, the story of the man born blind. From then onwards no mention is made of 'after that' until 19:38, after the death of Christ. It occurs again at the beginning of chapter 21, which exegetes agree is a later addition. As the first sign had already been reported in the Gospel's description of the first week, the first 'after that' is the only one that is not linked with a sign. But from the second 'afterwards' on, the text can run smoothly on its rails: each section beginning with 'after that' relates a sign, the second section relating the second sign, the third section the third sign and so on; moreover, each 'after that' introduces new characters and new journeys.

However, in the long sequence beginning in chapter 7, a new principle of ordering time is introduced. Now, Jewish feast-days are mentioned as time-indicators. John had already referred to the Jewish Passover (2:13) immediately before the incident in the temple, to a nondescript feast when he comes home to Galilee (4:45), and to the coming Passover at the multiplication of the loaves (6:4). Their import seems to be theological rather than historical. In the fourth Gospel Jesus, who will die at the Passover time, is indeed the bread of life and the new temple. From 7:1 however, the Jewish feast-days seem to become the only indications of time, while remaining reminders of the theological depth of the events. After the feast of Tabernacles (7:2, 14 and 37) and the feast of the Dedication, Jesus calls Lazarus back to life. In the last week of his life, which culminates at Easter, Jesus goes to Bethany 'six days before the Passover' (12:1); the next day (12:12) he enters Jerusalem in triumph; on a rather vague day 'before the Passover' the Last Supper is eaten, and Jesus dies on the eve of the Passover (19:31). Mary of Magdala discovers the empty tomb on the eighth day, 'the first day of the week' (20:1).

The reader is thus confronted with two types of chronology. On the one hand, there is the historical arrangement of the events in which each episode is given its sign; on the other hand, there is the theological urge which insists on placing Jesus' activity in a theological perspective. Relating Jesus' life in terms borrowed from the Jewish religion means that it can get its full meaning only through the relations of contrast and/or similarity obtaining between them. Moreover, it cannot be fortuitous that this Gospel begins and ends with the events of one week. These two weeks obviously 'rhyme' – that is, they are characterized by differences and similarities. The parallels between Cana and the cross are a case in point.

It is on the basis of these data that this reading of the Gospel is organized; how it works out can be seen in the Table of Contents.

The Narrative Point of View

A second point deserving attention is the narrator's time perspective. Theoretically, he can take up various vantage points; he may pretend that he is witnessing the events and is unaware of their outcome, or he may organize his narrative from the point of view of one for whom the story belongs to the past. John is always mixing the two perspectives. What is still in the future for the participants in the story, belongs to the past as far as John is concerned: he knows; they do not. He writes from the fullness of faith; they are slowly discovering it. What is unusual here is that John expresses this fullness; in long speeches, he contrasts the human view which develops in time with the divine one which is eternal. Once again, the tension between a historical perspective and a theological perspective makes itself felt. Whereas the former is subject to time and change, the latter remains eternally the same. That contrast shows in many episodes of the Gospel. One expects new information at each new episode, and what one actually finds there is remarkably similar to what was found in the previous episode.

Take the journeys of Jesus: he comes and goes, back and forth between Jerusalem and Galilee; he manifests himself and at the same time goes into hiding; he is threatened by his enemies and yet is invulnerable. During his first stay in Jerusalem, many believed in him, but 'Jesus did not trust himself to them' (2:24); when he is there for the second time, he heals the lame man and 'had withdrawn' (5:13). After the multiplication of the loaves, he 'withdrew again to the hills by himself' (6:15). Afterwards he refuses to stay in Judea, but then goes up to Jerusalem 'not publicly but in private' (7:10); yet he preaches in public. He is threatened by the Jews who want to arrest him, 'but no one laid hands on Him' (7:30).

From that moment onwards, the rhythm intensifies: 'Some of them wanted to arrest him, but no one laid hands on Him' (7:44). Some time later, in the Temple, 'but no one arrested him, because his hour had not yet come' (8:20). When they try to stone him, 'he hid himself and went out of the Temple' (8:59). A similar remark occurs at the end of Chapter 10: 'Again they tried to arrest him, but he escaped from their hands' (10:39). Finally, after the raising of Lazarus, 'Jesus no longer went about openly among the Jews, but went from there to the country near the wilderness' (11:54); and, to conclude, after he has announced his death, 'He departed and hid himself from them' (12:36).

A clear pattern emerges. Although there is a chronological progression with one event occurring after the other, the structure of the events is always the same. In the conflict between him and the Jews, Jesus must speak out openly in order to manifest himself, and he must go into hiding in order to avoid being taken prisoner. John gets out of this quandary by making Jesus both vulnerable and invulnerable. He projects the invulnerability of the risen Christ on to the historical Jesus. He can do that thanks to his supra-temporal vantage-point which he combines with the point of view of the participants in the story. His Gospel elucidates one basic proposition: 'The Word has become flesh.' That leaves open the choice between a concentration on the process of becoming – which would justify a chronology – or a concentration on the tension between the terms 'Word' and 'flesh' – and that would demand a thematic and structural approach. John wavers between the two approaches.

This is confirmed by his treatment of three other themes: the place where Jesus belongs, the meaning of his words, and his relation to the Old Testament. As far as the place is concerned, there is an ambiguity. After his ironical words to the Jews, 'You know where I come from' (7:28), he repeats, with a slight variation, 'Where I am you cannot come' (7:34; compare with 8:21). That makes sense only if he can be said to be both here (where his audience can see and hear him) and elsewhere at the same time; and that is what Jesus will actually aver: 'You are from below, I am from above; you are of this world, I am not of this world' (8:23). Texts such as these show that the narrator fuses the final situation when Christ has risen and is with God, beyond the reach of man, and the temporary situation where he is among us as a potential sufferer. In John's Gospel Jesus is both with the Father and on his way to the Father; he is at the same time the suffering man and the risen Lord, revealed and not yet revealed, in the world and out of this world, transfigured and not yet transfigured.

That also shows in Jesus' language which his enemies, and sometimes his friends too, fail to understand. He uses everyday words, popular speech: about the destruction of the temple (2:19–21), about birth in his conversation with Nicodemus (see ch.3), about water in his meeting with the Samaritan woman (see ch.4), about bread in chapter 6, and so on. Although these words are clearly intended to communicate a message, they seem at the same time to obscure it. The hearers are put on the wrong track because they are unaware of the fact that Jesus makes use of different levels of speech at the same time. His words both hide and reveal his message.

As for the Old Testament, that remains mysterious for the participants in the story. They cannot see its relevance for an understanding of Jesus. But after the Resurrection the light will dawn for them and they will discover what it means. There are, then, once again two perspectives in the Old Testament: in a historical perspective its truth or its relevance is not easily grasped but is discovered in a slow and sometimes painful progress; in a theological perspective the meaning of its words has always been clear.

The analysis of the time structure and the point of view has revealed the co-existence within the one Gospel of two attitudes to time. On the one hand, there is an awareness of the historical situation and the progression of faith, but on the other hand, there is also the certainty of an eternal truth which is always present. That has deep repercussions on our understanding of the Gospel, for it can lead to two readings. One could, for example, read the story of Nicodemus as one of the stages in Christ's self-revelation, but one can also read it as a typical instance of the relation between man and Christ. The historical reading, which locates this moment in time, offers one interpretation, the typological one offers another. They need not be mutually exclusive.

2: THE USE OF REPETITION

In the Prologue:

1:3   All things *were made* through him
       and without him nothing *was made* that *was made*.

1:4–6 In him was *life* and the *life* was the LIGHT
       and the LIGHT shines into the **darkness**
       and the **darkness** has not overcome it.

1:10   He was in the *world* and the *world* was made
        through him, yet the *world* **knew him not;**

1:11   he came to HIS OWN home
        and HIS OWN people **received him not.**

In the conversation with Nicodemus:

3:16   For God so loved the world
        that he *gave his only Son,*
        that whoever believes in him
        SHOULD NOT PERISH but **have eternal life.**

3:17   For God *sent the Son*
        NOT TO CONDEMN the world,
        but that the world **might be saved** through him.

3:18   He who *believes* in him IS NOT CONDEMNED;
        he who *does not believe* IS CONDEMNED.

3:20   For everyone *who does evil*
        HATES THE LIGHT and does not COME TO THE LIGHT
        lest **his deeds be exposed.**
        But he *who does what is true*
        COMES TO THE LIGHT
        that it may be **clearly shown that his deeds** have
        been wrought in God.

3:31   He who comes *from above* is ABOVE ALL;
        he who is of **the earth** belongs to **the earth,**
        and speaks of **the earth;**
        he who comes *from heaven* is ABOVE ALL.

3:36   He who *believes* in the Son has eternal LIFE
        he who *does not obey* the Son shall not see LIFE.

In Jesus' self-defence in relation to the cripple:

5:19   *The Son can do nothing* of his own accord

but only what he sees THE FATHER DOING;
for whatever THE FATHER DOES, *the Son does.*

5:21   For as the Father *raises the dead* and *gives life*
to them,
so also the Son *gives life* to whom he will.

5:22   The Father *judges* no one
but has given all *judgement* to the Son
that all may HONOUR the Son
even as they HONOUR the Father.
He who does not HONOUR the Son
does not HONOUR the Father who sent him.

In the discourse on the bread of life:

6:39   And this is *the will of him* who sent me
that I should lose nothing of all that he has
given me
but **raise it up at the last day.**
6:40   For this is *the will of my Father*
that everyone who sees the Son and believes in him
should have eternal life
and I will **raise him up at the last day.**

6:53   If you do not *eat the flesh* of the Son of man
and DRINK HIS BLOOD,
you have no life in you;
6:54   he who *eats my flesh* and DRINKS MY BLOOD
has eternal life,
and I will **raise him up at the last day.**

In the parable of the Good Shepherd:

10:14   I *know* MY OWN and MY OWN *know* me;
as **the Father** *knows* me and I *know* **the Father.**